Dreams from a Summer House

A musical play

Book and lyrics by
Alan Ayckbourn

Music by
John Pattison

Samuel French — London
New York - Toronto - Hollywood

DREAMS FROM A SUMMER HOUSE

First presented at the Stephen Joseph Theatre, Scarborough on 26th August 1992 with the following cast of characters:

Robert	Dale Rapley
Amanda	Janie Dee
Sinclair	David McAlister
Chrissie	Christine Cox
Grayson	James Tomlinson
Mel	Judith McSpadden
Belle	Jan Hartley
Baldemar	Anthony Venditti

Directed by Alan Ayckbourn
Décor by Juliet Nichols
Lighting by Jackie Staines
Musical direction by John Pattison

MUSIC

The vocal score is available separately (on sale) from
Samuel French Ltd.

CHARACTERS

Robert, an artist
Amanda, his ex-wife
Sinclair, Amanda's second husband
Chrissie, her mother
Grayson, her father
Mel, her sister
Belle, a beauty
Baldemar, a beast

SYNOPSIS OF SCENES

ACT I   A warm evening in summer

ACT II   An hour or so later

The action takes place in an English garden in August and beyond

Plays by Alan Ayckbourn published by Samuel French Ltd

Absent Friends
Absurd Person Singular
Bedroom Farce
Callisto 5
A Chorus of Disapproval
Communicating Doors
Confusions
A Cut in the Rates
Ernie's Incredible Illucinations
Family Circles
Henceforward ...
How the Other Half Loves
Intimate Exchanges (Volume 1)
Intimate Exchanges (Volume 2)
Joking Apart
Just Between Ourselves
Living Together
Man of the Moment
Mixed Doubles (*with other authors*)
Mr A's Amazing Maze Plays
Mr Whatnot
My Very Own Story
The Norman Conquests
Relatively Speaking
The Revengers' Comedies
Round and Round the Garden
Season's Greetings
Sisterly Feelings
A Small Family Business
Suburban Strains
Table Manners
Taking Steps
Ten Times Table
This Is Where We Came In
Time and Time Again
Time of My Life
Tons of Money (*revisor*)
Way Upstream
Wildest Dreams
Wolf at the Door (*adaptor*)
Woman in Mind

ACT I

The garden of the Huxtables' house. It is a warm evening in summer. Dusk has not yet fallen

Tall trees and thick shrubs, a rough lawn, perhaps a paved pathway, suggesting a well-established, big garden belonging to a large house, though the actual building we never see

What is in view is a good-sized wooden summer house complete with raised veranda. This is a building intended for guests to stay in. It probably has, in all, two or three rooms. On the veranda itself, there is a small garden table and two or three chairs. There are at least three ways of approaching this section of garden; from the main house, from the further reaches of the garden and from the summer house itself

There is at least one large tree and high up in it, reached by a rope ladder, a small tree house

At the start there is no-one in sight. The only evidence that the summer house is occupied is an unfinished water-colour illustration pinned to a board on the table and a few artist's accoutrements

Birds are singing their evening chorus though tonight they have competition for the Huxtables are holding a summer party. In the distance a small band, possibly a quartet, is playing soft "early evening" music. Background accompaniment to start the proceedings. Presumably it is intended that things will hot up later on. Occasionally, guests' voices and laughter can be heard. Perhaps the splash of one of them using the pool

A second or two to establish the scene until at length Mel, a girl of seventeen, creeps on from the direction of the house

A boyish, rather unkempt figure, she suggests someone who, rather later in life than most, is still at an emotional crossroads; no longer a girl but reluctant as yet to come to terms with her womanhood. She carries a pile of buffet food which has been hastily wrapped in paper napkins. Mel approaches the veranda of the summer house, moving carefully, anxious not to be discovered. She approaches the table and stares at the picture. She picks it up to examine it more closely. It is an illustration of Beauty and the Beast, presumably intended for a children's book. Two figures with Beauty clearly defined in all her stunning idealized female glory; Beast, on the other hand, lurks half unseen in the shadows

Mel wrinkles her nose in disapproval. She is clearly unimpressed by this artistic effort

From off stage, suddenly, we hear the sound of Chrissie, her mother, approaching

Chrissie (*off, from the distance*) Robert! Robert!

Mel darts hastily into the summer house to get rid of her food parcel. She re-emerges and thinks about escaping

Before she can do so, Chrissie appears. She is dressed for the party and looks very elegant. At present, though, she is rather agitated. Always a busy hyperactive person, some recent occurrence has sent her into virtual overdrive

(*To someone behind her, as she enters*) No, I'll do it. I'll do it. You look after the guests, darling ... Just take care of people ... (*Seeing Mel*) Oh, Mel, there you are. What are you doing here? Where's Robert?

Mel shrugs

Where is he? Is he here? Is Robert in there?

Mel shrugs again but still doesn't reply. Chrissie goes past her and to the doorway of the summer house. Mel moves away during the next and starts to climb up into her tree house

(*As she does so*) I need to speak to him. Something terrible's happened. It's absolutely catastrophic. (*Calling*) Robert! Are you in there?

She listens briefly

I mean, I don't know what we're going to do. We've got a hundred guests out there, practically the whole of Leatherhead, clamouring to be entertained, the caterers have only brought half the things we asked them for — I think Meryl must be having some sort of nervous breakdown, she's usually so well organized — and the band's arrived without their singer. (*Calling again*) Robert! Where on earth is the man? Has he gone out? How can he possibly have gone out? Where can he have gone to? He's supposed to be working. He can't have gone to the pub, surely? No. He promised me faithfully he wouldn't. He wouldn't go near that pub, I know he wouldn't ...

She stops to examine the picture briefly. Mel is now perched in the tree

Oh, this is charming, isn't it? Utterly delightful. He's so — so completely talented, isn't he? If only he'd ... sober up and pull his socks up he'd probably be a genius. Where is the wretched man? Where have you gone? Mel? (*Looking up and locating Mel*) Oh, darling, just look at you! You're just a walking mass of total and utter — frightfulness. Now Melinda, listen, I'm warning you, if you intend to come to this party, you will wash, you will comb your hair, you will change into proper clothing and you will try to give at least a passable imitation of a civilized female being ... I mean, look at you. I sometimes think I gave birth to a gibbon. Heavens, girl, at your age I was dancing and — coming out and ... (*vaguely*) ... so on ...

Grayson, Chrissie's husband, is heard calling her

Grayson (*off, nearby*) Chrissie! Chrissie!
Chrissie (*rather irritably*) What is it, dear?

Grayson appears, also a bit harassed. He hates these occasions — at least the organizing bit

Grayson The woman wants to know where we've put the Highland Spring Water.
Chrissie The what?
Grayson The Highland Spring Water. The woman can't find it.
Chrissie Who can't find it?
Grayson That woman. That catering person. Nerys.
Chrissie Meryl. Grayson, for the tenth time, her name is Meryl. It's in the fridge. In the big fridge. I told her that.
Grayson The big fridge?
Chrissie The big *downstairs* fridge.
Grayson The big *downstairs* fridge?
Chrissie She knows that. Not the big *upstairs* fridge.
Grayson (*doing his best to follow this*) No ...
Chrissie And not the *small* fridge downstairs.
Grayson No ...

Chrissie The *big* fridge downstairs.

Grayson The *big* fridge *downstairs*, right. I'll tell her.

Chrissie There's no point in telling her. She knows already, for heaven's sake. She put it in there herself.

Grayson Yes, well, I'll tell her anyway. Jog her memory. It's only for dear old Reggie, you see. He can't drink it any other way, poor chap. Single malt and Highland Spring. You know dear old Reggie.

Chrissie Indeed I do, I do. God knows I know dear old Reggie. I also know poor old Susie who has to live with dear old Reggie. But that's another story, isn't it?

Grayson (*going*) Yes. Right, I'll tell the woman. What was her name again. Myrtle?

Chrissie (*after him*) Meryl. Why can't the wretched man drink wine like everyone else?

Grayson (*as he goes*) Oh, come on, darling, fair do's. He doesn't ask for much, does he?

He goes off

Chrissie (*calling after him*) Only because he's barely capable of speech ... And do keep people away from the edge of the swimming pool, darling, won't you? We certainly don't want a repetition of last year. Just wait a minute and I'll ... (*To herself*) Dear heaven, what's the point of paying people if you finish up doing it all yourself? (*To Mel*) Mel, if Robert comes back, tell him I need to speak to him urgently. At once. And, darling, please, do at least wash your face. It's not too much to ask. Once a year, that's all.

Chrissie bustles off again

Mel watches her impassively. She gives a grunt and a brief Neanderthal impression, more for her own amusement than anything. She slides down her rope to the ground, thinks about leaving, then returns to the veranda and the picture. In the distance, the music plays on, a selection of apparent "standards". Mel sings softly to herself as she studies the picture

Mel (*singing, half inaudibly*)
> ... We rode our love like
> We would a subway train.
> Made every stop
> Vowing not to meet again ...

From the direction of the far garden, Robert appears quietly. He is holding a carrier bag. He sees Mel and stops to watch her

Mel is glowering at the picture. She takes up a pencil and is about to deface Beauty

Robert (*softly*) Try it and I'll break your arm.

Mel looks up, see Robert and puts down the pencil

(*Moving to her*) Well? What do you think of it?

Mel Terrible.

Robert Thank you. Just the sort of thing that would appeal to kids, do you think?

Mel It wouldn't appeal to anybody ...

Robert (*unaffected*) Really? Oh dear.

Mel Especially not kids.

Robert Ah well, you should know.

Mel Kids have taste. This is just sentimental crap, isn't it?

Robert Well, idealized romanticized crap, perhaps ...

Mel What's it meant to be?

Robert What's it look like?

Mel The Rape of Lucrece?

Robert Good guess. Hard luck. Try Beauty and the Beast.

Mel Which one's meant to be Beauty?

Robert Hey, kid, look at the time. It's way past your beddy-byes.

Mel You once told me you were a serious artist ...

Robert Time you were climbing that wooden hill, little lady ...

Mel You told me once you'd sooner starve than produce commercial garbage. I'd sooner starve, you said ——

Robert Well, that was before I got hungry.

Mel Got thirsty more like ...

Robert (*cautioning*) Ah-ah!

Mel I never believed you would, you know ...

Robert 'Night, 'night ...

Mel Sell out. Just sell out like this. After all that big talk.

Robert Look, there's nothing wrong with children's books ...

Mel I know ...

Robert There is a long, noble and distinguished tradition illustrating books for children ... Mabel Lucy Atwell to name but three ...

Mel Agreed.

Robert Well, then.

Mel (*indicating the picture*) So what's this mean to them then? Presumably a break with the long, noble distinguished tradition?

Robert does not reply

He takes up the picture and looks as though he might start work on it. Mel eases off the subject

By the way, I nicked you some food. From the party. I put it in there. On your kitchen table.

Robert *(ignoring her)* Thanks.

Mel I knew you wouldn't go to the party.

Robert Dead right.

Mel You need something to eat, don't you? Help soak up the alcohol.

Robert *(innocently)* Who's drinking?

Mel What's in the bag, then?

Robert Urgent medical supplies. Now piss off and go and play with a mains cable somewhere, there's a good child.

Mel Don't get defensive. I care what happens to you, that's all.

Robert Thank you, Milly Molly Mandy ...

Mel I care about your art, even if you don't ... I care about — you — drinking yourself to death.

A slight pause

I heard you. Last night. We all heard you.

Robert Heard what?

Mel You singing to yourself. Out here. Twenty past three in the morning it was.

Robert Was I? You sure it was me? I don't remember.

Mel It would be a miracle if you did. I'm amazed you can hold a paintbrush.

Robert You're growing up to be remarkably like your big sister, did you know that? Strident and repetitive.

He pretends to study his picture. Mel studies him

Mel You're pathetic these days, aren't you?

Robert ignores her

You used to inspire me, you know. When I was ... when I was younger. I thought you were ...

A pause

You know, I used to be jealous of Amanda. I was actually jealous. At your wedding. Did you know that? Standing there in that ghastly salmon pink bridesmaid's dress she made me wear. Jealous of my own sister. Not because ... nothing like that. Not what you're thinking, at all.

A pause

Now I pity her. Living with you. How did she put up with it? All those years?

A pause

Five years, was it?

Robert (*muttering*) Four and a half. Four years, one hundred and sixty-one days ...

Mel You should never have got married, anyway. I could have told you. There was no way you two would ever have ... I could have told you that for nothing. If you'd ever bothered to ask me.

A pause

Not that you'd ever take my advice, would you? You never listen to me. You treat me like a kid.

Robert (*growling*) You are a kid.

Mel I'm not. I'm seventeen years old. I'm a woman ——

Robert (*sharply*) Then for God's sake behave like one!

Mel is stung into silence. Robert is a little surprised himself at the force of his outburst

(*Rather more calmly*) You're a mess. You're a — walking rubbish tip, aren't you? Listen, seventeen-year-old girls — normal, healthy seventeen-year-old girls — most of them — they behave normally. They like to dress up occasionally — they want to make the best of themselves — they enjoy having their hair done — and sometimes — heavens! — they even put on make-up ——

Mel God, this is sexist ...

Robert They like to have boyfriends ...

Mel Have you any idea how old fashioned and sexist this is ... ? You sound exactly like my mother ...

Robert They even *wash* occasionally.

Mel What do you mean? I wash. I don't smell, do I?

Robert I don't know. Keep downwind of me, that's all.

Mel (*hurt*) God! The things you say to me sometimes. Honestly ...

Robert (*more gently*) Listen, Mel, seriously, all I'm saying is mature girls
— mature young women — usually tend to develop a little grace, a particle
of dignity, a modicum of poise. They don't run round bare-assed, wearing
their hair like an unwashed rat's nest, or spend their waking hours swinging
about in trees, all right? Now grow up. Your mother's right.

Mel is silent

You have to grow up, Mel. You want to be taken seriously, treated like an
adult, you've got to grow up.
Mel (*pondering this*) I don't spend my life swinging about in trees ...
Robert No? What's that then? (*He indicates the tree house*)
Mel Where?
Robert There? Up there? What do you call that?
Mel What's wrong with having a tree house?
Robert Nothing ...
Mel Well, then.
Robert Not for twelve-year-old kids. It's great. But it's a little incongruous
for a seventeen-year-old woman.
Mel God, you've really got it in for me today, haven't you?

Robert laughs

You've really shocked me, you know. You've really deeply shocked me.
Robert How come?
Mel All that bit about women. Women do this, women do that ... it's so boring
and conventional and — masculine.
Robert So? I'm a man. Sue me.
Mel Not that sort of man you aren't. At least I hoped you weren't. I mean,
for someone your age, you seemed practically enlightened.
Robert What age?
Mel You know, middle-aged ——

Robert looks dangerous

(*Amused*) Sorry, sorry. Early middle age. Terribly early middle age. Now
look at you. Sitting there painting soft porn for kiddies.
Robert What are you talking about? Soft porn?
Mel What else do you call that? You're just perpetuating existing sexual
stereotypes, that's all you're doing ...
Robert Where do you get all this jargon? Off a cornflakes packet?
Mel Well, look at it. Just look at her ...

Robert If you're referring to Beauty here, she's — beautiful. I won't hear a word against her.

Mel She's a tart. A male fantasy. All she needs is a staple through her navel. Who is she, anyway?

Robert No-one. I'm a creative artist. I dreamt her up, didn't I? Why?

Mel I thought she might be one of your ex-girlfriends. You've had one or two of those in your time, haven't you? I'm sure you can paint them from memory.

Robert Mind your own business.

Slight pause

What is it? Jealous that I haven't asked you to pose, are you? Asked you to pose for Beauty?

Mel I will if you pose for the Beast.

Robert You could, you know.

Mel What?

Robert Pose. Seriously.

Mel Don't be funny.

Robert You could.

Mel What, as Beauty?

Robert You could look pretty good. If you put your mind to it.

Mel (*hardening*) How kind of you to say so. So could you.

Robert Now who's getting defensive ...

Mel (*moving away, angrily*) If that's all you want from me, just get stuffed ...

Robert That's not all I want from you ...

Mel Go and buy yourself a girly calendar ...

Robert I wasn't meaning in the nude, for God's sake ——

Mel Better still, get yourself one of those inflatable dolls.

Robert Mel ...

Mel If she gets too threatening for you, you can always let the air out of her, can't you?

Mel goes off into the far garden

Robert (*after her*) Mel ... (*To himself*) Kids, I don't know ...

He is rather annoyed with himself for the way he's dealt with her. He shrugs, and reaches into the carrier bag and takes out a new bottle of Scotch. He breaks the seal and, emptying the contents of a jam-jar full of old paint water, pours himself a stiff drink. He puts away the bottle again

(To the picture) You're beautiful, all right? Don't let anyone tell you otherwise ... Here's mud in your eye, Beauty.

He toasts her. The music in the distance plays on. Robert sings along with it for a moment

(*Singing to himself*)   Senorita,
                         Pretty Senorita
                         Won't you whisper
                         Spanish words of love ...

He is awoken from his reverie by the sound of Chrissie's voice from the direction of the house

Chrissie (*off, approaching*) Robert! Robert!

Robert hastily puts down his glass and grabbing a paint brush, wiggles it about in the Scotch, turning it a muddy grey

   Chrissie appears

Robert, there you are. Where have you been? Have you heard?
Robert Heard what?
Chrissie Nobody's told you? You haven't heard?
Robert No.
Chrissie They're back.
Robert Who's back?
Chrissie Amanda. Amanda and Sinclair. They phoned from the airport. Just half an hour ago. They're back in England.
Robert But they're on their honeymoon.
Chrissie They were.
Robert For a month.
Chrissie They were.
Robert In Italy.
Chrissie Yes, they were, they were ... only Sinclair ...
Robert Don't tell me. She shot him?
Chrissie No, of course she didn't.
Robert He shot her? Better still ...
Chrissie No, no, no. They're both passionately in love, don't be so silly ... (*She is by the picture looking at it again as she speaks*) I used to have a dress rather like that ——
Robert Really?
Chrissie I never looked quite as good as that in it, alas ...

Robert (*gallantly*) Nonsense.

Chrissie It's frightfully good ....

Robert Thanks.

Chrissie (*sniffing around the paint jar suspiciously*) What's this smell?

Robert Paint.

Chrissie Really? No, anyway, there is apparently some urgent business deal come up and Sinclair's had to hurry home. What sort of paint?

Robert Oil paint.

Chrissie Oh, yes? Anyway, they'll be back here at any minute ...

Robert What fun ...

Chrissie And if Amanda finds you here ... I thought you used water-colours ...

Robert Yes, I do. Oil-based water-colours ...

Chrissie Oh, yes? I mean, Sinclair's not exactly going to be over the rainbow to see you either, is he?

Robert What's it got to do with him?

Chrissie Oh, come on. His bride's ex-husband. Not the sort of person you want waiting for you when you're freshly glowing back from your honeymoon, is it? I mean, you're my favourite man in the entire world but you're simply going to have to go, Robert.

Robert Go?

Chrissie Now.

Robert Now?

Chrissie At once.

Robert I'm not leaving now.

Chrissie You must.

Robert Why should I? You invited me here.

Chrissie I know that. I know I invited you. Only I didn't know they were coming back now, did I? I mean, when I invited you to use the summer house I assumed they'd be away for — weeks. But now ... You know what Amanda's like. She'll be just as impossible if she finds you. Beside herself with fury. And, as you well know, she is quite frightening when she gets like that. She frightens me, anyway.

Robert She frightens everyone.

Chrissie She does, she does. I know. I can't think where she gets all that frighteningness from, I'm sure. I mean, I'm not frightening, am I?

Robert Not at all ...

Chrissie Her father isn't. Grayson's not frightening, is he?

Robert No, he certainly isn't. He's alarming sometimes, but not frightening.

Chrissie No, there's nothing for it, you'll have to leave now, Robert. Pack your things. We'll smuggle you out the back.

Robert is absently sipping his paint water

Robert I'm not sure I can agree to this, you know, Chrissie. I mean, after all, I — I mean, fair's fair. I'm halfway through a commission. And we did have an agreement ... (*He takes another swig*)

Chrissie You haven't started drinking again, have you, Robert?

Robert What? (*He puts the paint-water jar down again*) No.

Chrissie Because that was also part of our agreement, wasn't it? I mean, you promised me, didn't you? You did promise me.

Robert Yes, I did. And likewise you promised me I could stay here and work in peace. What happened to that promise?

Chrissie Now, that is totally unfair ... You really can't hold me to ——

Grayson enters with his glass

Grayson Hallo ...

Chrissie (*rather snappishly*) What is it now, darling?

Grayson It's — er ... that woman again. Cherith ...

Chrissie Cherith?

Grayson No? Cheryl? Getting warmer? Beryl?

Chrissie I presume you mean Meryl?

Grayson Meryl, that'll do it.

Chrissie (*to Robert*) He runs this vast empire. Thousands of employees, he can't remember a single name. Not one. He can barely remember mine. How does he cope?

Grayson I cope perfectly well. I call them all Martin.

Robert Martin? What about the women?

Grayson I call them Martin as well. It doesn't seem to bother most of them. If it does, they leave, I don't care. No skin off my nose.

Chrissie What's the problem?

Grayson What problem?

Chrissie You just said there was a problem. What was it?

Grayson No idea. Oh yes, what's-'er-name's crying.

Chrissie Crying?

Grayson In the middle of our marquee.

Chrissie What? *Our* marquee?

Grayson 'Fraid so.

Chrissie Why? Why is she crying?

Grayson Haven't a clue. Something to do with pastry.

Chrissie Pastry?

Grayson Well, she's totally legless, you know.

Chrissie Drunk?

Grayson Drunker than Reggie and that's saying something ...

Chrissie Poor, poor old Susie. (*Setting off*) I don't believe this. How are the guests taking all this?

Grayson Oh, they're just milling round, you know. Treading on her. Pretending not to notice. I say, aren't Amanda and Sinclair due in a minute?

Chrissie (*indicating Robert*) Just persuade this man to leave. I want him out, Grayson. Out now. Do you hear?

Grayson Right.

Chrissie And tell him not to drink, either.

She goes

A silence between the two men. Grayson hums along with the band for a moment

(*Singing to himself*) ... my girl's — simply the cat's pyjamas ...

Robert takes out the Scotch bottle. Grayson tips away his glass of white wine on the grass and accepts a Scotch. Robert replaces the bottle in the carrier bag

(*Raising the glass*) You heard her. Don't drink. And get the hell out of here. Cheers. (*He drinks*)

Robert Cheers.

Grayson No, seriously. You shouldn't do it, you know. Not at your age. It's very bad for you. Look at Reggie. Drinking since he was a baby. Now he's got the mind of a child.

Robert (*taking a swig*) Good advice, father-in-law. Ex-father-in-law, I beg your pardon. I'm going to miss you, you know. I'm going to miss our chats together.

Grayson So am I. Hardly going to be the same with Clinton, is it?

Robert Sinclair.

Grayson Sinclair. (*Saying it over to himself, pottering around*) Sinclair, Sinclair, Sinclair. I mean, he's a lot better for Amanda, far better than you ever were. But he's a hell of a lot worse for me, I can tell you. (*Looking at the picture*) This is good.

Robert Thanks.

Grayson She's got a fine chest on her.

Robert Think so?

Grayson Very well drawn.

Robert Thank you.

Grayson Almost feel you could — reach out and touch it, don't you? Very realistic. Follows you round the room, doesn't it? I could never draw a chest like that. Not in a hundred years. Do you mind my asking, is it based on anyone in particular, or ... ?

Robert No. Off the top of my head.

Grayson You don't mind my asking?

Robert No.

Grayson (*sadly*) Never gone in for chests much, in our family. Any of them. Chrissie, Amanda. As for Mel ...

Robert (*suddenly defensive of her*) Mel has — other qualities ...

Grayson Can't beat a good chest, though, can you? Not on a woman. Beats everything else into a cocked hat ...

Robert Now that's not politically correct talk, Grayson. Not these days. You'll have Mel after you, talking like that ...

Grayson I don't care if it's correct or not. All I'm saying is, that in my humble opinion as a mere male, when it all boils down to it, as far as women are concerned, you have to go a long way to beat a cracking good pair of knockers.

Robert There really is no answer to that.

Grayson That's all I'm saying. Just one man's opinion. No offence intended. What's this for then? Playboy?

Robert No. A children's book, actually.

Grayson A children's book?

Robert Yes.

Grayson What? For children?

Robert Yes.

Grayson To look at?

Robert Yes.

Grayson My God. (*Slight pause*) Oh, to be young again, eh? (*He laughs*)

A pause

(*Singing to the music again*) ... my girl's — simply the cat's pyjamas ... (*Speaking*) I like this one. Mel's always playing it. What's it called?

Robert Er ... It's called "We Can Save the Trees" — something like that.

Grayson Is it really? Where do the cat's pyjamas come into it then?

Robert I don't think they do.

Grayson Ah, well. I only hear it through the floor, so ... Listen, personally I'd love to sit and talk to you all night, but you're really going to have to leave, you know, I mean, you mustn't think us rude but ...

Robert No. Quite.

Grayson There'll be the most God-awful row otherwise, won't there? If Amanda finds you here. You must understand that, surely?

Robert (*depressed*) Yes, you're right. Of course. I'm not wanted here, I can see that.

Grayson I mean, if I had my way ...

Robert I'll go and pack.

Grayson (*anxiously*) Are you sure?

Robert Sure. I'll go and bed down on the river bank. It's a lovely evening. Why not?

Grayson I feel awful turfing you out like this. If it weren't for these bloody women, I'd ...

Robert Grayson, in a perfect world, there wouldn't be any bloody women. Well, none like that. There'd be only perfect girls with vast chests and unfailingly sunny dispositions. Girls who are there solely to whisper, "I love you, I love you, I love you. For ever and ever and ever and ever". But the world isn't perfect, I'm afraid, is it? Instead it is filled with lean mean, narrow-eyed, suspicious, sanctimonious, flat-busted women with lantern jaws and the light of sexual battle eternally in their eye. Women who mean us all harm and humiliation. Who take the bread from our mouths and snatch the bottle from our lips. Women who argue with us just for the joy of putting us down. Who laugh at us just for the sheer pleasure of watching us grow smaller and smaller by the minute. And they, Grayson, they eventually inherit the earth. Not us. Not you and me. For they are the stronger sex. Not, you understand, the better sex but the stronger one. And you and I will be crushed to dust beneath the platform heels of their aerobic, biodegradable trainers. For lo and behold, it is writ, blessed are the titless — for they shall inherit the earth. And frankly, Grayson, just between you and me, just at this moment, they're welcome to it.

A slight pause

Grayson (*slightly taken aback*) Well, I don't think I'd put it quite as strongly as that. Don't worry. I'll get someone to drive you to the station. I'll arrange that. There must be someone here who's still sober. Some poor bloody woman driver sipping orange juice ... I'll tell you what. I'll let you have the key to our flat in town. How about that? It's quite small but you can put up there temporarily. Just till you get yourself fixed up ——

Grayson breaks off as they hear a loud splash from the direction of the house followed by a great commotion

What the hell ... ?

Robert Someone's fallen in the swimming pool by the sound of it ...

Grayson (*laughing*) Good Lord, so they have. I wonder who — Oh, my God, it's Reggie! It's dear old Reggie! He'll sink like a stone. Excuse me, I must ...

Mel enters and is moving towards the house

Grayson in his haste almost collides with her

I'm so sorry. I do beg your pardon, I — (*Seeing who it is*) Oh, hallo, Mel. Where are you off to?

Mel (*grimly*) I'm going to miraculously transform myself.

Grayson You are?

Mel Into a cheap tart.

Grayson I beg your pardon?

Mel Why not? It's what everyone would prefer, isn't it?

With a sidelong glance at Robert, she stomps off

Grayson stares after her, mystified

Grayson Extraordinary beings, aren't they? (*Looking off again*) My God, I think he's just come up for the third time. Do excuse me.

Grayson hurries off

Robert watches for a moment, initially amused until the pall of gloom settles over him once more. He sighs. He dives into the carrier bag again, removes the Scotch bottle and takes a swig. He bangs the bottle rather noisily down on the table. He snatches up a grip bag from under the table. Into this he starts to throw his artist's equipment rather haphazardly. Having completed his task, he pauses, tosses the grip back inside the house and takes up the Scotch bottle again. He stares afresh at his picture

Robert (*to the picture*) The trouble with you is, my beauty, everyone's jealous of you. That's the problem for us beautiful people. Always been my problem. In my case, a beautiful soul. What I want is someone who can appreciate a man with a deeply beautiful soul, that's all. Preferably a deeply beautiful woman.

He takes another swig. Then another. Once again he begins to hum along with the off-stage band, in between sips of liquor. His singing gets a little louder. He starts to sing the words to the tune of what is presumably some standard that the band are playing

(*Singing, half to himself to start with*)
                    It's merely academic I
                    Recall the things I do,
                    Those vows of everlasting love we swore,
                    That overwhelming happiness
                    When I was close to you —
                    I didn't think it meant much any more

He gets a bit tearful. The drink and the sentiment are mixing badly. During the following, he gathers up a few bits and pieces

> For we change — thank the Lord —
> We mature, we get wise.
> And how strange, we walked around with
> All that moondust in our eyes.
>
> It's solely for my record books
> I think of you at all,
> The way you walked, your smile, the clothes you wore,
> Each second that I spent with you,
> Each glance, however small —
> I didn't think they meant much any more.

He goes into the summer house. Almost at once, as from nowhere, Belle appears looking every bit as beautiful as her image drawn by Robert. She seems literally to have stepped from the pages of a story book. Robert's rather rowdy, drunken singing continues

(*Off*)   Now you're here,
> There's that moon throwing dust in my eyes.
> And it's clear my so-called wisdom's
> Based on nothing more than lies ..

Robert emerges and now sees Belle for the first time. He gapes at her

> Here we go, once again,
> Look who's here. Big surprise.
> Should have known a love like ours was
> One that never really ... (*He tails away*)

Robert stares at Belle. Belle stands looking a little bewildered. Robert smiles

Hallo. I don't believe we've ... Have we? I'm sorry, I'm Robert Gates. And you're — er ... (*Staring at her harder*) No. We have met. Yes, we've definitely met — now where? Where? Where? Where? Let me try and guess. You're at the party, right? Yes, obviously. This is fascinating, don't tell me. I always remember ... Eventually. Especially someone ... Especially someone like you. You're not a friend of my ex-wife's? No. No way could you be a friend of my ex-wife's. Wait a minute, it's coming, you're ... (*He looks incredulous*) You're ... You're ...

Robert slowly picks up his picture and compares the two, Belle and his own drawing

(*Softly*) My God. It's exact. It's uncanny. (*He stares at her afresh*) We must have met. That's the only solution. I met you before. A long time ago. I've forgotten the meeting — how the hell did I forget that meeting — but I've carried your image in my head all these years and I just ——

Slight pause. He looks at the Scotch bottle

No more. That's it, I tell you. That is it. Move over, Reggie. It's Highland Spring water for me.

Pause

Who the hell are you? Are you real? Can I touch you? No, I don't want to touch you. If I touch you, you'll turn into my ex-wife. All women do. It's my curse. One touch, I turn warm, decent, loving women into my ex-wife ... Do you understand what I'm saying? Do you even speak English? Hey, listen, please do me a favour. Either de-materialize, turn into a pink elephant or speak to me. Please ...

The following is now sung unless indicated

Belle (*softly*)   Help me ...
Robert (*speaking*) What?
Belle (*urgently*)   Help me ...
Robert (*speaking*) Help you?
Belle   Robert, will you help me?
Robert (*speaking*) How? I don't know what you mean ——
Belle   Help me ...
Robert (*speaking*) Tell me! How? How can I help you?
Belle   Robert, will you help me?
Robert (*speaking*) We don't seem to be getting very far, do we? (*Loudly and clearly*) Do you understand me? Speak you English?
Belle   Help me!
Robert (*speaking*) I've got it. I know who you are. You're the missing vocalist with the band, right?
Belle   Help me!
Robert (*speaking*) You're a musical kissogram? That'd be nice.
Belle   Help me!
Robert (*speaking*) You're singing on behalf of charity? How much do you want?

Belle   Help me!

Robert (*speaking*) OK, you've made your point, it's a great song but I give
up. You'll have to tell me, sorry.

Belle (*a musical cry of frustration*)
                             Aaaah!

Robert (*drily*) Yes, yes. That's very good. (*Copying her, singing*)
                             Aaah!

Belle (*brightening up, responding*)
                             Aaaah!

Robert (*speaking*) Oh, you like that, do you? You like duets? (*Singing*)
                             Aaaah!

Belle (*responding*)   Aaaah!

Robert (*speaking*) You want me to sing to you? (*Singing*)
                             Aaaah!

(*Speaking*) Like that?

Belle   Aaaah!
Robert   Aaaah!
Belle   Aaaah!
Robert   Aaaah!
Belle (*a high and mighty note*)
                             Aaaaaaaaah!

Robert opens his mouth to respond and thinks better of it

Robert (*speaking*) No, sorry, I can't — (*Correcting himself, singing with
difficulty*)
                             I can't get right up there. No way!

Belle   Would you like me to come down the octave?
Robert (*with strain*) Please do.
Belle (*down in pitch*) Is that better for you?
Robert (*down with her*)
                             Much better. Thank you.
Belle   You're welcome.
Robert   I can't believe this is happening ...
Belle   Help me! You have to help me.
Robert   But how do you get to be here, anyway?
Belle   I escaped. I've run away.
Robert   Escaped from where? Who from?
Belle   It's a long story ...
Robert   Try me.

(*Speaking*) Though I've a nasty suspicion I know where you've escaped
from ...

Belle   What's that?

Robert	Nothing, tell me.
Belle	All right. Here goes.
	Once upon a time,
	My rich merchant father
	Gathered a rose that belonged to a creature,
	A creature known as Baldemar,
	The Beast.
	The Beast he grew angry
	He vowed to kill my father,
	Only agreeing to spare him his life
	On condition that my father gave to him instead
	His youngest, most beautiful, loveliest, charmingest daughter.
	Me!

Robert (*speaking*) Yes, I know all this already, I read the book.

(*Singing*)	I read the story.
Belle	The story? It's a story?
Robert	It's an old, old story ...
Belle	It may be a story to you
	But for me it's my life ...
Robert	I'm sorry.

(*Speaking to himself, half under his breath*) Humour her.

(*Singing*)	I appreciate the problem.
Belle	Thank you.
Robert	If it's any consolation,
	You both live happily ever after.
Belle	How do you know that?
Robert	I read the ending ...
Belle	I wish I could feel that certain ...
Robert	I'm sorry. I interrupted you. Carry on.

(*Speaking to himself*) What the hell? Let's get certified together.

Belle	So I did obey
	Just to save my poor father,
	Went there to live in that dark empty castle —
	That castle owned by Baldemar
	The Beast.
	Each night he would call me
	To sleep in his bed chamber
	Every time I would run away and hide.
	Till the Beast became angry, locking me away
	Chained to a wall in a dungeon, with just bread and water —
	Me!

And sometimes he would plead with me.
Or coax with gentle words.
At other times he would starve me.
Or beat me.
Or curse me.
Or cosset me.
Or court me.
But when night fell,
I would never give myself,
Ever.
For never, never, never could I find it in my heart to love
    him.
The day came when I
Couldn't take it any more.
I ran away,
By doing so, I surely have condemned
My own father to death.
Robert, I'm so frightened.
I must go back to save his life —
Afraid to return there ...

Robert   How did you get here?

Belle is silent

But how did you get here?

Belle   There must have been a link, I suppose ...

Robert   A link ... ?

Belle   There has to be a link to get from where I live
To — where we are.
It must be you.
It must be you ...

Robert   Me?

Belle   Something between us
Somehow our needs
Were the same.
It's so hard to explain ...
No-one fully understands.
All that we know
Is that someone's need must be so great
So overwhelming
Someone answers their call,
Someone from the other side.

	All that I know is that
	You heard my cry.
	You were sent here to save me.
	Likewise,
	I heard your cry.
	I was sent to save you.
	Help me, Robert,
	I'll try my best to help you.
Robert	You're so beautiful.
	What is your name?
Belle	You know my name ...
	My name is Belle,
	Also known as Beauty ....
Robert	Beauty ...
	I am sleeping
	For it's when I'm dreaming
	I find Beauty
	That's the way it seems.
Belle	You're not sleeping.
	You can reach and touch me.
	Beauty's with you
	Stepping out of your dreams.
Both	If we're sleeping
	We must share this dream.
	Let's sleep for ever
	Ever more.
	Hold me tightly,
	Tightly in your arms ...
Belle	Here in the dark night
Robert	While you're sleeping
	I will keep you safely ...
Belle	You'll keep me safe while I dream of you ...
Robert	... sleep, sweet Beauty,
	Dream your lover's dreams.
Belle	... safe in my lover's arms

Belle is now close to Robert. He moves closer

Both	If we've woken
	Can this all be real?
	To find perfection's
	Not a dream.

Under the next, unseen by either, Chrissie enters. She stops short and stares in amazement

> Awake, asleep, let's stay inside our dream
> And fill our nights with love ...

They kiss deeply

Grayson joins Chrissie. He stares in equal amazement

Robert finally breaks from Belle. He sees the others for the first time. The following is now spoken unless indicated

Robert Ah, hallo.
Chrissie Hallo.
Grayson Hallo.

Slight pause

Robert This is — er ... This is ——
Chrissie Hallo.
Grayson Hallo, there.

Slight pause

(Sotto voce *to Chrissie*) Who is she?
Chrissie (*likewise*) I haven't the faintest idea.

They continue to smile at each other. Grayson is goggling at Belle

(*Rather coolly, to Belle*) Hallo ... I think you probably have the advantage. Robert, aren't you going to introduce us?
Robert (*uncertain*) Yes, of course.
Grayson I've met her before.
Chrissie Nonsense.
Grayson Definitely.
Chrissie I hope you haven't. Robert?
Robert — Er ...
Grayson We have. I recognize her ...
Chrissie Robert? Do introduce us.
Grayson I'm sure I'd never forget ... Never ...
Chrissie Grayson, don't boggle like that. It's terribly rude. Come on, Robert, please ...

Robert Yes. Well, this is — er, this is — Beaut — Belle — Princess Belle
— Princess Belle of — er ...

Grayson I don't think he knows who she is, either ...

Robert Princess Belle of Bolitzia.

Chrissie (*impressed*) Oh, a princess?

Robert Yes. An old friend. We ran into each other. Quite unexpectedly.

Chrissie (*all charm*) Well ...

Grayson Where the hell's Bolitzia ... ?

Chrissie Grayson! Don't be so ignorant. (*To Belle*) Honestly, you'd never
believe my husband runs a multi-national corporation, would you? He can
barely find his way to Guildford.

Grayson Well, where is it, then? Bolitzia? You tell me.

Chrissie Bolitzia? Well, it's — er ... It's over there. Isn't it?

Robert Way over there.

Chrissie Yes. Way, way over ...

Robert Precisely.

Grayson (*unconvinced*) Yes. (*Muttering*) I've met her somewhere, I know
I have.

Robert Unlikely. She normally moves in — very high circles.

Chrissie Welcome, Princess. It's a great honour to have you at our party ...

Belle does not respond

Robert Unfortunately, the princess speaks no English.

Chrissie She doesn't?

Robert Not a jot.

Chrissie Then how did she get here? Who invited her in the first place?

Robert Well, you see, her Rolls broke down ...

Grayson Broke down? That's unusual.

Robert In the road, just out there. And she — the princess who was on her
way to a royal reception — elsewhere — wandered in through the gap in
the hedge for a glass of water — and coincidence! Who should she run into
but me. An old friends from years back.

Chrissie Extraordinary. (*Beaming at Belle*) Hallo.

Grayson (*craning to see*) Where's her Roller now, then?

Robert The princess's chauffeur is pushing it to the garage.

Grayson What, the garage in the village?

Robert Right.

Grayson Up that hill?

Robert All the way.

Grayson Big chap, is he?

Robert Vast.

Chrissie Listen, everyone, what are we going to do with her? We can't let her stand out here in the garden all night, can we? (*Beaming again at Belle*) Hallo. (*Back to the others*) It's getting rather chilly. I mean, she's hardly dressed for — for standing about, is she?

Grayson Wait a second. I think I know where I've seen her before. Isn't she ... ?

Robert (*swiftly*) How's dear old Reggie?

Grayson Reggie?

Robert Your friend? Dear old Reggie?

Grayson Oh, dear old Reggie. Damp. But he's OK. I gave him a brandy.

Robert A change is as good as a rest.

Grayson His words exactly.

Chrissie (*loudly to Belle, slowly*) Would you care to come up to the house? *A notre maison? Notre petit château?*

Belle looks blank

Does she speak absolutely no English at all?

Robert Afraid not.

Chrissie Well, you seem to have managed to get along all right, if I may say so. How do you two communicate?

Grayson I'd have thought that was pretty obvious. Where did you meet her?

Robert Oh, years ago. While I was over there.

Chrissie I never knew you were over there.

Robert Just for a while.

Grayson You've kept pretty quiet about her ...

Robert It was years and years ago. Long before I met Amanda.

Chrissie I should hope so, too. If Amanda had ever clapped eyes on this one while you were both married, she'd have — My God! Amanda! What are we doing standing around chatting like this? She'll be here any minute. They were getting a taxi straight from the airport. Listen, Robert, Mrs Elms — you know the doctor's wife, Tommy Elms' wife — Vinny Elms? She has very kindly agreed to drive you to the station ...

Robert To the station? I thought I was getting a lift to London?

Chrissie There's no time to argue, please. Get your things together and go. Grayson, give him a hand. Quickly! Quickly!

Grayson Right. What have you got? (*Picking up Robert's bag*) Is this all there is?

Robert (*with ill grace*) There's a couple more things inside still to pack, I'll get them. The princess could have a lift with me. I can drop her off in the village.

Chrissie No, I wouldn't hear of it. She must stay here till her car is mended. You go.

Robert But I'm sure she'd prefer to ——
Chrissie Don't argue. Shift yourself. (*Smiling at Belle*) Hallo. Sorry about this, Your Majesty. Your Royal Highness ...

Robert goes into the summer house

Perhaps you'd care to shelter in our little marquee?

Belle smiles at her

Marquee. Uno mark-ee! (*She mimes*) In our tent. Tent. You see ...

Belle echoes her gesture, smiling

That's it. Jolly good. (*To Grayson*) She hasn't a clue what I'm talking about. I feel like Isadora Duncan ...
Grayson (*pottering on to the veranda, calling to Robert*) Don't forget your picture ... (*Picking it up*) Don't want to leave this behind, do you?

Robert darts out of the summer house and grabs the picture from Grayson

Robert Thank you.
Grayson Mind you, wouldn't worry me if you did. I wouldn't mind sticking it on the wall in my ... Hang on. Just a tick. Let's have another look at that ...
Robert Not now, we're in a hurry ...
Grayson But wait a minute ——
Chrissie Grayson, don't hold him up ——
Grayson No, but I've just remembered where I've seen her before. The princess.
Chrissie Where?
Robert Nowhere.
Grayson Yes, I have. I was trying to think. Where? Where? Where have I seen her before? I was trying to think. And I've just thought.
Chrissie Where? Where then?
Grayson I'm just telling you, in the ——

At this moment, the moon comes out. Belle decides to speak, or rather sing, for the first time in their presence

Belle (*singing*)   Oh, look. What a beautiful moon!

A stunned silence for a second

Chrissie I thought you said you didn't speak any English?

Robert She can't.

Chrissie Of course she can. She just spoke some. Beautifully.

Robert No, no, she didn't. She didn't speak.

Chrissie She did, I heard her. We all heard her.

Robert No. You heard her sing. She didn't speak.

Chrissie Speaking, singing, what's the difference?

Robert Oh, a great deal. I mean, if she ——

Chrissie Who is she?

Robert I mean, if you ——

Chrissie Robert, who is she?

Grayson I tell you, I know who she is. She's ——

Chrissie Grayson, just shut up a minute ...

Robert Shut up, Grayson!

Chrissie Robert, we heard her quite distinctly. Oh, what a beautiful moon, she said.

Robert No, no. She sang "Oh, what a beautiful moon".
  (*Singing*)   Oh, what a beautiful moon ...

Belle (*instantly responding in song*)
                        Isn't it? So romantic.

Chrissie There you are. She's just said something else.

Robert No, you see, she can sing English. But she can't speak English.

Chrissie What nonsense.

Robert It's true. It's the way they teach English — over there. They teach them languages by — getting them to sing.

Grayson Clever idea.

Robert Yes, isn't it? The only problem is — they can only speak a language when they sing it. And they can only understand it when it's sung to them. Useful at the opera ——

Grayson Or in the bath.

Robert Absolutely. Very progressive schooling, they have over there.

Grayson In Bolivia?

Robert Bolootsia.

Chrissie Bolitzia.

Robert Right.

Chrissie I've never heard such rubbish in my life.

Robert It's true. Try it and see.

Chrissie Certainly not.

Robert (*singing*) Princess, may I introduce,
                        My ex mother and father-in-law?
                        Chrissie and Grayson
                        Huxtable.

Belle (*singing*)   Hallo.

Grayson (*speaking*) Hallo.

Chrissie (*speaking*) Hallo.

Belle (*singing*)   Please call me Belle.

Chrissie (*speaking*) Thank you, Princess — Belle. And may I say that whilst you're in our house, please treat it as you would your own home. Our little residence is your little — residence. And could I just add, on behalf of all of us, welcome to Leatherhead.

Belle looks blank

Robert It's no good, she's no idea what you're saying. You have to sing it, if you want her to understand you.

Chrissie Oh, don't be so stupid ... This is some practical joke.

Robert (*singing*)   Welcome to Leatherhead!

Belle (*singing*)   Thank you!

Chrissie Well, I'm certainly not going to stand here singing at someone. I don't care if she is a princess, I'm sorry.

Grayson Oh, come on, Chrissie. Don't be such a spoil sport.

    (*Singing*)   Hallo!

Belle (*singing*)   Hallo!

Grayson (*singing*)   How do you do.

Belle (*singing*)   How do you do.

Grayson (*speaking*) There you are. Nothing to it.

Chrissie I'm not singing. I haven't sung since I was — I was in the kindergarten choir.

Grayson Rubbish. You've got a jolly nice voice.

Chrissie Not any more ...

Grayson You have. You're always warbling round the place ...

Chrissie Well, that's hardly the same as ——

The following is now sung unless indicated

Grayson   Princess, may I present my wife, Chrissie,
                               Who's an absolutely first-rate singer
                               Once she gets going.
                               But she's just a bit shy at the moment.

Belle   Hallo, Chrissie.
                               What a beautiful garden you have.

A silence. They all look at Chrissie

Chrissie (*uncertainly*) All things bright and beautiful
                               All creatures great and small ...

Belle (*puzzled*)	Where? I can't see any.
Grayson	Hark at my wife!
	She has this wonderful sense of humour.
Robert	Wonderful sense of humour ...
Grayson	Sense of humour ...
Belle	She's got a wonderful sense of humour?
Grayson	Sorry, Princess,
	It takes a little bit getting used to
Robert	A little bit getting used to ...
Grayson	Getting used to ...
Robert	But what a wonderful sense of humour ...

They all laugh, except Chrissie who looks rather put out by all this

Belle	Please tell me this,
	Why do you all keep referring to me as princess?
Grayson	Would you prefer a less formal address like Your
	Highness?
Belle	Hardly at all.
Robert	Of course, she's travelling incognito.
Grayson	Travelling incognito?
Belle (*puzzled*)	Incognito?
Chrissie	How thrilling! Travelling incognito!

She looks startled. The others stare at her

Belle	Please understand,
	I'm just an ordin'ry merchant's daughter.
Chrissie (*startled*)	Ordin'ry merchant's daughter?
Grayson (*likewise*)	Merchant's daughter?
Robert	Yes. He's one of the merchant princes.

They all laugh again

(*To Belle*)	Isn't that so?
Belle (*reluctantly*)	Well, in a way he's sort of a prince, yes in theory.
Robert	Royals, you know, find this title talk terribly dreary.
	Nevertheless.
	She's still a genuine royal princess
Grayson	Genuine royal princess!
Chrissie	Royal princess?
Belle (*startled*)	I'm a genuine royal princess?
Chrissie (*speaking*)	Then why did she say just now that she was —— ?

Robert	Wouldn't you know?
	She has this wonderful sense of humour.
Grayson	Wonderful sense of humour ...
Belle	Sense of humour ...
Chrissie }	
Robert }	What a wonderful sense of humour ...
Grayson }	
Belle	Well, fancy that! I never knew
	I had a wonderful sense of humour
Robert	Wonderful sense of humour ...
Grayson	Sense of humour ...
Belle	I've got this wonderful sense of humour.
Chrissie }	
Robert }	Yes, thank the Lord,
Grayson }	
All	We've all got a
	Wonderful, wonderful, wonderful, wonderful
	Wonderful, wonderful, wonderful, wonderful,
	Wonderful sense of humour!

They all laugh

*During the following Amanda and Sinclair appear. They stand watching
in some surprise. Amanda looks very disgruntled. They have obviously had
one hell of a journey*

Chrissie (*speaking*) Oh, this is rather fun ...
Belle (*not understanding her*)

	I beg your pardon?
Chrissie	Rather fun!
	Thank the Lord ...
All	Yes, thank the Lord,
	We've all got a
	Wonderful, wonderful, wonderful, wonderful
	Wonderful, wonderful, wonderful, wonderful,
	Wonderful, wonderful, wonderful, wonderful
	Wonderful, wonderful, wonderful, wonderful,
	Wonderful sense of humour!

*The others finish their chorus and see the new arrivals. The following is now
spoken unless indicated*

Amanda (*coolly*) Sorry to interrupt.
Chrissie Amanda! What a lovely surprise!

Amanda Surprise?

Chrissie Well, I meant ... Lovely! Now, we must introduce you — Amanda ...

Amanda If you're intending to re-introduce me to Robert, Mother, I'd sooner you didn't. More than anything else in the world, I'd sooner you didn't.

Robert (*cheerfully*) Hallo. Lovely to see you, too.

Chrissie No, of course I wasn't going to introduce you to Robert. I meant the princess. This is Princess Belle of Bolitzia ...

Amanda Princess who?

Chrissie Belle of Bolitzia.

Amanda Oh yes? Bolitzia? Where's that, then? The Isle of Wight?

Chrissie No, of course not. It's over there.

Grayson Way, way over there.

Sinclair Yes, I think I've heard of it.

Grayson Have you?

Sinclair Definitely. Passed through it, anyway. On the way to — somewhere else.

Chrissie The point is — Amanda, Sinclair ...
(*singing briefly*)   ... do excuse us, Princess ...

Belle (*singing*)   Certainly!

Chrissie ... when we need to address the princess we have to — sing to her. You see?

Amanda Sing?

Chrissie Yes.

Amanda You did say "sing"?

Chrissie Yes. Otherwise she can't understand us.

Amanda I see.

Sinclair Oh, right.

Chrissie (*singing*)   Princess, may I humbly present my son-in-law, Sinclair Platt.

Belle (*singing*)   Hallo, Sinclair Platt.

Sinclair (*singing along, cheerfully*)
                         Hallo, hi there!
(*He laughs*)

Chrissie And, Princess, may I also present my elder daughter, Amanda ... (*Remembering herself*) Oh, do excuse me. (*Singing*)
                         May I also present my elder daughter, Amanda Janet Dilys Ethel Seymore?

Belle (*singing*)   Hallo, hallo, hallo, hallo, hallo ...

Robert She has this wonderful sense of humour ...

Sinclair laughs. Amanda glares at him. An awkward silence

Chrissie (*nervously*) Do join in, won't you, dear? (*Whispering*) She is a princess.

Grayson (*whispering*) Mercantile.

Amanda (*icily*) I am not singing, Mother. I am tone deaf, you know that. Good-night.

Chrissie Where are you going?

Amanda (*dangerously quiet*) Mother, I am extremely tired. We have had a terrible trip back. A nightmare journey.

Robert (*singing, to Belle*)
                     She's had the most terrible journey ...

Belle (*singing*)   Too bad.

Amanda (*grimly ignoring them*) Quite frankly the sight of Robert was shocking enough ...

Robert (*singing*)   She's not too delighted to see me.

Belle (*singing*)   How sad.

Amanda And I'm certainly in no mood for party games and musical charades ——

Robert (*singing*)   She's not in the mood for a party ...

Belle (*singing*)   Oh, dear.

Amanda He shouldn't be here in the first place ...

Robert (*singing*)   I shouldn't be here in the first place ...

Belle (*singing*)   What, here?

Amanda Who invited him back into my life? You know I never wanted to see him again ——

Robert (*singing*)   She never again wants to ——

Amanda (*screaming*) Shut up! Shut up! Shut up!

They stop

    (*Pointing at Robert in a terrible fury*) —— It's all his doing! This is all his fault!

Robert Me?

Amanda (*pointing at Chrissie, accusingly*) Did you invite him here? You did, didn't you? This is all your fault ...

Chrissie Me?

Amanda Get him out of here! Get him out, do you hear? I want him out. Out! Out! Out!

Belle giggles, assuming this to be some sort of game

    (*Wheeling on Belle*) And tell him to take that plastic simpering —— thing with him ——

Belle retreats behind Robert

Chrissie Amanda, please! Darling, please.

Amanda (*apoplectic with fury*) This is all her fault! I want her out! Out! I want them both out! Get them out!

Chrissie Grayson! Somebody! Do something. Sinclair, slap her face, she's hysterical ...

Amanda Don't you dare touch me, Sinclair!

Sinclair (*nervously*) No, I'd prefer not to, if you don't mind ...

Robert I don't mind slapping her face ...

Amanda You try it! You try it! You try!

Chrissie Grayson, talk to her!

    (*Singing*)   Be right with you, Princess.

    (*Speaking*) You're her father. Talk to her. She listens to you.

Grayson (*ineffectually*) Yes, well, simmer down, there's a good girl ...

Amanda Don't you start, Father, this is all your fault ...

Grayson Righty-ho.

Chrissie Thank you, Grayson, you're such a help.

Amanda (*only a fraction calmer*) Here I am back from my honeymoon, we haven't even unpacked — well, we can't, can we, they've lost all our bloody luggage, haven't they? (*Pointing at Sinclair*) Which was entirely and totally his fault ...

Amanda moves away

Chrissie Where are you going, darling?

Amanda (*nearly in tears*) You're all to blame! I blame all of you for this. I'll never forgive you. Any of you!

She goes off into the far garden

Chrissie Oh dear. She's in an appalling state, isn't she? Worse than usual ... Oh, well, never mind. Can't be helped. Grayson, we must look after our guests ...

Grayson Oh, yes. I'd better nip up there and get them all singing, hadn't I? Warm them up for the princess. Reggie's got an awfully pleasant voice. Light baritone. Quite surprising for a man of his weight. He was in — er ——

Chrissie Yes, all right.

Grayson What was the one with all those gondoliers in?

Sinclair *The Gondoliers*?

Grayson That's the one.

Chrissie Grayson!

Grayson Yes, all right, I'm going.

Grayson starts to move off

Chrissie (*calling after him*) And tell Vinny Elms she can stand down. Robert is now staying ...

Robert Am I? Oh, splendid.

Chrissie You might as well, I suppose. The harm's done now, isn't it? Anyway, you've missed the train. You can stay on here in the summer house ... The princess can — she can have Mel's room. I'll get Mel to tidy it up. It's a wonderful excuse ...

Robert Oh, no. I mean where's poor Mel going to sleep?

Chrissie She can sleep in that tree house of hers. She does half the time, anyway.

Robert Oh no, that sounds like an awful lot of trouble. I'm sure the princess would be just as happy here, you know, mucking in with me in the summer house ...

Chrissie No, she wouldn't.

Robert I'm sure she would if you asked her. (*Starting to sing*)
                    Wouldn't you —— ?

Chrissie (*cutting him off*) Not while Amanda's here, she wouldn't. The princess stays in the house. You stay in the summer house. I'm not having a princess mucking in in a summer house and I'm certainly not having you mucking about under our roof ...

Robert It's OK, I can sleep up at the house. You'd never know I was there.

Chrissie Robert, Amanda would know you were there. That's the point. Think of poor Sinclair. What sort of a night would he have if she knew you were sleeping under the same roof as them?

Sinclair Quite. Think of other people.

Robert From the look of her, what sort of a night is Sinclair going to have anyway?

Sinclair I think I'll muck in in the summer house as well. (*He laughs*)

Chrissie No, it's all settled. Princess, would you care to — Sorry. (*Singing*)
                    Princess, would you care to pop up to the house to —
(*Speaking*) This is most awfully difficult. They can't have many secrets from each other, can they? Everyone trilling away ... (*Singing*)
                    ... Go into the house to tidy up?

Belle (*eagerly, singing*)
                    Of course, I'd love to.
                    Your house needs tidying?
                    I'd simply love to.
                    I'd love to see inside and tidy up
                    Your little wooden house.

She runs into the summer house excitedly

Chrissie (*calling after her*) No, for heaven's sake, we don't live in there — (*To the others*) She obviously has a rather lowly view of our social status.

Belle (*off, singing*)   Oh, this is lovely.

Chrissie Well, I suppose she's trying her best. Robert, will you bring her up
to the house, as soon as possible? Explain to her that we're just driving the
cattle out of the bedrooms ... Sinclair, I think you should go and look for
Amanda.

Sinclair (*unenthusiastically*) Oh. Do you think so?

Chrissie Yes. I do.

From off stage the sound of massed rather drunken tuneless singing

Dear God. What is Grayson doing? That's enough to drive the poor woman
straight back to Bolitzia. Up at the house, Robert. With the princess. Two
minutes. (*To Sinclair, as she goes*) Find Amanda.

Chrissie goes off to the house

The singing continues under the next

Sinclair I don't think I'll try and find her just yet. Give her another ten
minutes.

Robert I'd have thought at least that. If she's on form, she'll just be coming
out of ungovernable fury and entering deep depression mode.

Sinclair Do you think there's something wrong with her?

Robert Yes.

Sinclair No, I meant medically?

Robert Yes.

Sinclair Could be, you know. She's always getting into these states.
Happened all the time on the honeymoon. All the time. On the hour. Day
and night. Especially night. (*To Robert*) Was she like that on yours?

Robert Not at night. I managed to shut her up at night.

Sinclair Did you? How did you — ? Oh, I see. That. You got around to that,
did you? Lucky chap. More than we did.

Robert No, we didn't get around to that either. I just used to lock her in the
wardrobe.

Sinclair (*laughing*) Good idea. I never thought of that. Seriously though, I
mean, she's a terrific person — don't get me wrong — but I think she's
someone who sets pretty high standards.

Robert For herself?

Sinclair No, for other people mostly. And the problem is — the real problem
is — that most of us absolutely fail miserably to live up to her standards.
I certainly do. The result being she's pretty well continually in a constant
state of hairlessness. Does that sum her up, do you think?

Robert Very accurately. She's also a selfish cow ...

Sinclair (*admonishingly*) Ah, now. Come on, come on. This is my wife we're talking about. Watch it.

Robert I'm sorry.

Sinclair Watch the language. I mean, she may be hell to live with occasionally but she's still my wife and I won't have a word said against her, all right?

Belle comes out of the summer house. She has on an apron and holds a duster

The following is sung unless indicated

Belle	... I love your little house. It's very like my home ...
Robert	(*speaking*) Yes, Belle ... (*Singing*)
	Belle
Belle	I love the little room in which it rains ...
Robert	No, that is a shower ...
Belle	It seems more like a downpour.
	(*Frowning, listening*) But what is that?
	The sound of many people all so miserable ...
Robert	No they're not miserable.
	That's the sound of the English
	Enjoying themselves.
Belle	How simply terrible.
	I ought to carry on
	It badly needs a clean
	I'll make it spick and span,
	Your little wooden house.

She goes back inside

Robert (*after her, in vain*)
                    Belle ...
(*Speaking, to Sinclair*) I must just go and sort her out.

The following is spoken unless indicated

Sinclair Yes, I'd better go and hunt for ... (*Looking after Belle*) You've got hold of something a bit special there, haven't you?

Robert I think so.

Sinclair Princess-cum-charwoman. Can't be many of them about. Ideal combination, really.

Robert (*going inside*) See you in a minute.
Sinclair Absolutely.

Robert goes off

Sinclair stands rather aimlessly, obviously not too keen to go off in search of Amanda

(*Calling rather softly*) Amanda! Amanda! Amanda! (*He listens for a second*) No. She's obviously not around.

Mel comes on from the house. She has undergone a remarkable transformation. She is now done up to the nines in an elaborate party dress. She has obviously made a great effort for Robert's benefit

Under the next, the drunken singing from the house stops fairly abruptly

(*Failing to recognize her for a second*) Hallo. Mel? Yes, it is. Hallo, Mel.
Mel (*a bit self-conscious*) 'llo.
Sinclair You look — you look — very different. Different from usual.
Mel Glad you noticed.
Sinclair Yes, I did.
Mel Is Robert in there?
Sinclair (*vaguely*) Yes, he's just ... I'm just going to beat the bushes for my wife. Excuse me.

Sinclair wanders off, apparently in no great hurry

Mel approaches the summer house. She braces herself for the big impression she is hoping to make

Mel Hi! You in there?
Robert (*off*) Just a second, I'll be right with you.

Mel arranges herself

Robert comes out

Sorry, I was —— (*He sees Mel and breaks off*)

A pause. He is impressed

Well. My God. Yes. I think you've made your point. You look — fabulous.

Mel It's all right, I didn't come for compliments. I just did this in order to prove how easy it is for anyone, even me, to ——

Belle appears beside Robert in the doorway. She still has on her apron and is holding her duster

They look an idyllic couple. Mel stares at her. Belle smiles back radiantly

(*Stunned*) Oh.
Robert Ah. This is — Mel, this is Belle.
Mel (*dully*) Hi.
Robert (*singing*)   Belle, meet Mel ...
Belle (*singing*)   Hallo, Mel. How good to meet you ...
Mel (*covered in confusion*) Yes. Excuse — Excuse me.

Mel dashes back towards the house, passing Chrissie as she does so

Belle looks puzzled

Chrissie Oh, Mel — I need you, I wanted to — (*Calling after her*) Mel! Melinda! Really, I don't know what's the matter with these girls. (*Staring after Mel*) Those are my ear-rings. (*To them both*) I came to fetch you. Are you ready?
Robert Yes, we're just coming. Here.

He helps Belle to remove her apron, taking the duster from her

Chrissie What on earth has she been doing?
Robert Just — trying on some things. She wanted to see what it was like to wear an apron. The common touch.
Chrissie Oh, well, I could have told her.

Chrissie returns her attention towards the party, momentarily

At least they've all stopped singing. That's a relief. The neighbours called the police. It could have been very ugly. I tried to explain to this sergeant it was for a royal occasion, but ——

The following is sung unless indicated

Belle (*to Robert*)   Who was that girl who ran away?
Robert   Oh, just a kid ...
Belle   She looked to me to be a woman
                             Who is deeply unhappy.

Robert	Yes, well, all the women are a bit miserable round here. Come on!
Belle	Where are we going?
Chrissie	To our house. Over there.
	Can you see? Through the trees?
Belle	That's your house? Over there?
	Oh, dear Lord ...
	It looks very like his appalling castle ...
Robert	It's what we call Mock Tudor.
Belle	What a fearful place ...

Belle and Robert go off

Chrissie (*speaking, rather hurt*) Yes, well, we do our best. Be it ever so humble there's no place like half a million pounds worth of home counties real estate ... (*She is about to go*)

The following is spoken unless indicated otherwise

Amanda wanders back from the far garden

Oh, there you are, darling. Have you cheered up a bit?

Amanda glares at her

Obviously not. You're going to have to do something about yourself, you know, darling. You're just permanently glum these days. In a complete gloom, aren't you? When you're not in a filthy temper ... It's so miserable for you. Not to mention everyone else. I mean I hate to say it, but there are times you're just impossible to live with.

A slight pause

Amanda (*rather meekly, for her*) You really think so?
Chrissie What?
Amanda That I'm impossible? To live with?
Chrissie Well. I don't have to live with you these days, of course. But all these poor men. I mean, I really do feel for them sometimes.
Amanda (*flaring*) Who? Who are you talking about? Are you talking about Robert and Sinclair?
Chrissie Yes, I suppose I am. Primarily. There are all those other poor little creatures you frightened away, of course, but really I suppose I am — I'm talking about Robert and Sinclair.

Amanda But they're all so—useless, Mother. I mean, they're so completely useless. No, it's not just those two. I don't want to sound unreasonable. It's all men. They're all useless. I mean, name me one man who isn't, in the end, useless. Name one.

Chrissie Well, I suppose it depends to what use you want to put them, doesn't it? I mean, your father ... Yes, I have to admit it, in one respect, he is utterly useless. But he's quite fun. Sometimes. He was. And he's ... he's ... I don't know, he's sort of nice to have around, isn't he? I mean ... I don't know ... (*She trails off rather lamely*)

Amanda Mother, listen to yourself. You're not talking about a man. You're talking about a dog. If you're just looking for something that's fun and nice to have around, then go and buy a dog and a rubber ball. At least you'd know where you were, then. You wouldn't sit there hoping that one day it might just do something remarkable. Amusing. Affectionate. Considerate. Thoughtful. Masterful. Yes, even masterful. You know, sometimes, I think I'd even settle for a man that bullied me. Bossed me around, occasionally. Told me what to do. Made decisions. Didn't leave everything, every little tiny thing, eternally, entirely to me. Mother, there has to be a man somewhere who's got some sort of inner strength. One you can actually lean on once in a while. One who's not a complete and utter, spineless wimp.

Sinclair wanders on at this moment

Sinclair (*seeing Amanda*) Oh, there you are ...
Amanda (*very fiercely*) Go away!
Sinclair (*not too upset*) Yes, OK.

Sinclair goes off again in the same direction

Chrissie I think you're going to have to sort this one out for yourself, dear. Nothing I can say is going to help, is it? Yes, you're right. Men are probably all the things you say. They're generally hopeless and occasionally quite appalling. You just have to learn to live with them, darling. Because unfortunately they're here to stay. You just have to learn to — live round them. That's what I do. Build a by-pass.

Chrissie goes out

Amanda, on her own, remains deeply unhappy. She meanders on to the veranda rather aimlessly. She picks up the picture that Robert has left there. She studies it. She scowls

Her first instinct is to hurl it deep into the bushes. But she controls herself with a great effort and puts it down again quite gently. She is overcome with a wave of depression

Amanda (*with a great cry*) Oh, what am I going to do? Someone, somewhere, help me! Please!

There is a low rumbling sound slowly building in volume. Everything seems to shake. The lights from the garden and those from the summer house flicker

Something approaches from the far garden

(*Peering into the gloom*) Who is it? Who are you? Who's out there?

Suddenly, Baldemar the Beast emerges from the bushes

Amanda screams

Baldemar advances on her and traps her before she can escape

(*Agitatedly*) Get away! Get away! Get away from me!

She gives another squawk as Baldemar seizes her and effortlessly heaves her across his shoulder. He is evidently immensely powerful. Amanda wriggles in vain

As Baldemar starts to make off the way he came, the others rush on from the house but are too late to stop him. First Chrissie, then Robert and Belle, Grayson and finally Mel. Simultaneously, from the other direction, Sinclair enters. He is nearly knocked down by Baldemar as he exits with the squawking Amanda

Chrissie (*arriving*) Amanda, darling! What's happening? Sinclair, do something ... !
Amanda (*as she is carried off*) Mother, help me! Please, help me!
Sinclair (*during this*) Good grief! Put her down! Do you hear me? Put her down this instant! What do you think you're doing?
Robert (*a fraction after them*) Amanda! What the hell is it? Amanda! (*To Sinclair*) Come on! After them!

Robert, with Sinclair a few paces behind him, make to follow Baldemar and Amanda

Belle arrives

Belle (*singing*) Oh no, no, no. No. No ...

Grayson (*arriving*) I say — what's all the din? My God, who is it? Is that her chauffeur?

Mel (*arriving, softly to herself*) What is it? What is it?

Robert and Sinclair go off briefly

Chrissie That was the most terrifying thing I've ever seen. What is it? What was it?

Grayson (*calling after the two men*) Any sign of them ... ? Looks as if he's making for the road. Cut him off! Tackle him. Bring him down!

Chrissie No, don't bring him down, he's carrying Amanda ...

Sinclair returns breathlessly carrying one of Amanda's shoes

Grayson You haven't given up, have you?

Chrissie How pathetic!

Sinclair (*barely able to speak*) Vanished ... just vanished ... in a cloud of dust ...

Chrissie Vanished?

Grayson Rubbish!

Robert returns

Chrissie Well?

Robert Sorry. He got away. Disappeared into thin air.

Grayson How could he, man? Damn great thing about nine foot tall carrying a substantial quantity of woman ... ? Absolutely impossible just to disappear.

Robert Impossible unless ... (*Looking at Belle*) Unless ... (*Singing*)
                     Who was it? Was that — ? Belle?

Belle (*singing*) That was —
                     That was the vile creature I was once betrothed to marry.

Chrissie ⎫
Robert ⎬   Marry?
Grayson ⎭

Chrissie (*speaking*) That was never her fiancé, surely?

The following is sung unless indicated otherwise

Belle   Now he believes you have stolen his bride
                     So, in his revenge, he takes yours ...

Sinclair   Taken her where?

Belle   Who knows?
Chrissie   What will he do?
Belle   Who knows?
Grayson   What is his name?
Sinclair   What is his name?
Chrissie   What is his name?
Robert   Tell them!
Belle (*very distressed*) Who knows? Who knows? Who knows? Who
                     knows!
    (*A scream*) Who knows!

Belle stands, her hands to her head. They all look at her. A pause

Robert (*gently*)   Princess, tell them ...
Belle (*reluctantly*)   His name is Baldemar,
                     Also known —
    (*Almost a whisper*)   Also known as The Beast ...

The others stand horrified as the music surges and darkens

Sinclair collapses in a faint as ——

                     — the Lights fade to BLACK-OUT

ACT II

The same. An hour or so later

The band is still playing in the distance

After a moment, Grayson enters from the direction of the house

Simultaneously, Robert and Sinclair come on from the direction of the far garden. They have apparently been searching for Amanda. Sinclair has a small tree branch he has been using for "beating"

Grayson No?
Robert No.
Sinclair No.
Grayson No.

A silence

Absolutely baffling. Agatha Christie stuff, eh?
Sinclair Yes.
Grayson (*to Robert*) It's beginning to look like yours is the only possible explanation, Robert.
Robert It is.
Grayson Bit hard to swallow, though. If you don't mind my saying so.
Robert I agree. It is.
Sinclair It's downright ridiculous.
Grayson So. Let's get it straight. This woman ... Belle, also known as Beauty, she runs away from this chap Balzac ——
Robert Baldemar ...
Grayson Baldemar — also known as The Beast and she comes running to you. Why to you?
Robert I think — it's hard to explain — but by some strange coincidence — I happened to be concentrating on her — on Belle's visual image — at the exact moment Belle was trying to escape. I somehow provided the link.
Grayson The link?
Robert From — where they live to — where we live. They live — somewhere altogether different from us, you see ... We don't even exist in the same time ... So very rarely do the two of us connect. Certainly not

physically. Mentally, occasionally, we do — we pick up fragments of their history — visual images — hence all our fables and fairy stories — they're all essentially true ...

Grayson True?

Robert So Belle says ...

Sinclair What, Babes in the Wood? Mother Goose ... ?

Robert Apparently. She's not been too sure about The Wizard of Oz but the rest of them really did happen. She's actually met Snow White, you know. She's quite an old woman now but she's still very active.

Grayson Social worker, no doubt.

Sinclair Oh, come off it. This is all a load of utter blatherskite and you know it. There's a far more logical explanation for all this. There must be.

Robert What?

Sinclair I don't know. Let's give it a moment's thought, shall we?

A silence

Amanda's living with the seven dwarfs?

Grayson (*doubtfully*) Well, in the absence of a slightly more coherent prognosis, let's accept — as a working marginal hypothesis — the far flung possibility of Robert's theory being remotely correct. And I'm putting it no more strongly than that.

Robert Fair enough.

Grayson So. What have we got? She runs here to you. Balshazzer gets fed up and comes after her and snatches Amanda instead. Takes her back there to — well, let's face it, a place we'll have to call for want of a better word — Fairyland. There I've said it. So. We now have Amanda in Fairyland — which I have to say does make the mind boggle a bit — so the question is — how do we get her back? Indeed, is it possible to get her back?

Robert Do we even want her back?

Sinclair Now, I'm warning you, Robert, that's enough of that ...

Robert I'm sorry, Sinclair ... Well, the thing is that two of you, one on each side, have to be mentally and emotionally attuned to make the link ... Belle needed to escape badly enough. And I obviously responded in some way to her — with a need of my own. Baldemar similarly needed to come here to find Belle. While Amanda ... (*He hesitates*)

Sinclair Amanda?

Robert She obviously wanted ... she wanted ... I don't know what she wanted, Sinclair. Who knows with Amanda? She's your wife. You tell us. She was obviously sending out some sort of signal, anyway, and Baldemar latched on to it.

Sinclair Well, say it. A distress call. That's what it was, wasn't it? Mayday, Mayday.

Robert I wouldn't say that, I ——

Sinclair (*suddenly very distraught*) Oh, look, this is appalling. I've lost my wife, can't you see that? My new wife. I'd only just married her. She was brand new. (*He is in tears*) What are we going to do?

Robert moves away slightly, finding this rather embarrassing

Grayson Steady. Steady on, Sitwell ...

Sinclair (*weeping openly*) I love her, you see ...

Grayson Yes, yes ...

Sinclair I mean, I know one shouldn't say these sort of things out loud, but I can't help it. I love her. It's an awful, embarrassing thing to say and one shouldn't say it ...

Grayson No, it's not an awful thing to say, not at all. You say it ...

Sinclair I shouldn't be saying it, I know I shouldn't. I'm sorry.

Grayson No, what the hell, you say it. A chap loves his wife, damn it, it's a rare enough thing these days, virtually unique, he's entitled to say it. Go on, yell it out, Simpson, get it off your chest ...

Sinclair (*shouting*) I love her.

Grayson Good man. Well done. That's better.

A slight pause

Sinclair (*more in control, sadly*) I don't think she loves me, though.

Grayson Now, we don't know at all ...

Sinclair I think we do, you know.

Robert She doesn't love anyone, Sinclair. She never has done.

Grayson (*inclined to agree*) Well ...

Sinclair recovers a little

Sinclair I say — would it be in order to ask that band to stop playing that dreadful jolly music? I mean, I'm finding it a bit inappropriate ...

Grayson (*doubtfully*) Yes ...

Sinclair Everyone's gone home. There's no point in them playing, anyway.

Grayson Well, they've been paid until two o'clock, you see. I'd rather like to get my money's worth if I could. They weren't cheap, those chaps. It's only for another twenty minutes.

Robert Perhaps we could ask them to play something more suitable ...

Grayson You mean, a gloomy foxtrot or something? Well, I could try it out on them ...

Robert I was thinking more of "Happy Days Are Here Again" ...

Sinclair (*angrily*) One more joke like that, Robert, I'm warning you ...

Robert I'm sorry, Sinclair.

Sinclair (*agitatedly*) Why aren't we going to the police? We should be going to the police.

Grayson You want to ring them? Excuse me, officer, I have reason to believe my wife has been carried off to fairyland by a nine-foot monster. Fancy your chances with that one, sunshine? They've been to this house once tonight as it is. Threatening to book a hundred people for singing while drunk and disorderly. They're not in the best of moods. I'd forget that one.

Sinclair (*in despair again*) Well, what are we going to do?

Chrissie and Belle enter

Chrissie No sign of her?

Grayson No. Everyone gone home, have they?

Chrissie Yes, last one's just left. Your friend dear old Reggie. Dragged out feet first by poor old Susie.

Grayson Did you manage to explain to everyone about Amanda.?

Chrissie Yes, I said she'd — suddenly gone down with something ...

Sinclair (*emotionally*) My God!

Grayson Samson here, I'm afraid, has got a bit depressed.

Chrissie Who?

Sinclair Sinclair ...

Chrissie Well, none of us are exactly leaping about with joy, are we? We're all — (*a glance at Robert*) — most of us are very upset. Poor Sinclair ...

Sinclair Thank you.

Chrissie Belle's just been singing to me though, Sinclair, that Amanda's not in any physical danger. So that's a relief, isn't it?

The following is sung unless indicated

	Amanda's not in any danger, is she?
Belle	She will come to no harm
	For despite how he looks,
	Baldemar will not kill her or hurt her.
	He may lock her away
	He may starve her for days
	He may threaten and shout just to scare her.
Sinclair (*speaking, appalled*) Oh, my God ...	
Belle	But under the provisions of the witch's curse
	He can make life impossible but not much worse ...
Chrissie (*speaking*) Well, a sort of mixed bag in a way.	
Belle	He can shut out her light,
	He can turn off her heat,

He can flood half her dungeon with water
Or infest her with rats
Or with spiders and lice,
In the end it's decreed he must spare her.

Sinclair (*speaking*) This is appalling ...

Belle   For under the provisions of the witch's spell
He can do little more than make her life sheer hell ...

Chrissie (*speaking*) Well, really no worse than that frightful boarding school she went to.

Belle   For despite all his threats
It remains her own choice
As to whether she yields or resists him.
For he knows in the end
He can't take her by force
If she goes to his bed she'll go freely.
For under the provisions of the witch's charms
She must go to him willingly with open arms
For under the provisions of the witch's hex
She'll discover with Baldemar a perfect, perfect ——

The following is spoken unless indicated

Chrissie (*coming in very crisply*) There you are, you see, Sinclair. There's nothing to worry about, is there?

Sinclair (*even more depressed*) Oh, my God ...

Chrissie Now, follow me everyone, there's a mountain of food to finish up. Including a delicious sherry trifle. Come on, otherwise it'll only go to waste. (*Singing, to Belle*)
                    Sherry trifle!

Belle (*singing*)   Sherry trifle! (*To Robert*) What's sherry trifle?

Chrissie This poor child, she knows absolutely nothing. She wandered round all our guests in a complete daze. And I've never seen anyone get so excited about a waste disposal.

Grayson (*to Sinclair*) Come on, old chap, look on the bright side. For all we know she might be having the time of her life.

They all go off towards the house

Sinclair What sort of consolation is that? (*Turning as they go*) Amanda! Where are you? Come back to me ...

They go off

There is a crash of music and the Lights change to something rather gloomier and unreal

The summer house veranda becomes the mouth of a dungeon in Baldemar's castle. This is achieved instantaneously, ideally with light alone, as we will move to and fro from this quite a lot

Baldemar enters with a bowl of food. He grunts to himself

He reaches the dungeon entrance and bangs the bowl on the ground. He grunts and bangs it again

A clanking sound from within the dungeon and Amanda appears. Her dress is torn, her face is grimy. Round her neck is a large steel collar. Attached to this and trailing off behind her is a length of business-like metal chain

Amanda ... about time, too.

Baldemar makes some indecipherable grunting noises indicating that she should eat

What? What are you saying?

Baldemar repeats his instructions

I'm sorry, I don't know what you're talking about. Will you kindly take this thing off me at once and let me go.

Baldemar makes a threatening move towards her, growling

(*Rather alarmed*) Don't you — don't you dare ... Don't think you're going to get away with this. My husband is — my husband can be very dangerous. If he's roused. You'll be sorry if you don't ——

Another threatening growl

What is it? What do you want? You want me to eat that? (*She inspects the bowl, suspiciously*) I'm not eating that. What is it? You can't expect me to eat that. Well, at least provide me with a knife and fork. Knife and fork. Knife and — God, he doesn't understand a word I'm saying. This is impossible. (*Calling*) Sinclair! Anybody! Mother! Robert! (*To herself*) God, no, not Robert. (*Calling again*) Anyone but Robert! Please!

The following is sung unless indicated

Baldemar (*suddenly*)   You are my prisoner.
                            And here you will stay!
Amanda (*speaking, startled*) What? What was that?
Baldemar   No-one can save you
                            Submit to your destiny!
                            Frail woman, you are mine to command!
                            Resign yourself to a fate
                            Worse than death!
Amanda (*speaking*) Oh, dear heaven. He's a madman.
Baldemar   Still your tongue, foolish maiden!
                            Your words are as empty air!
                            If you would speak to me,
                            Like the cagéd nightingale,
                            You must learn to sing for me.
Amanda (*speaking*) Oh, no. I am not singing for you or anyone, I'm sorry.
    You can forget that straight away ...
Baldemar   Sing for me ...
Amanda (*speaking*) I'm sorry, I am not singing ...
Baldemar   Sing for me ...
Amanda (*speaking*) I refuse to sing, do you hear me?
Baldemar   Sing for me ...
Amanda (*yelling*) For the last time, I refuse to sing. Get that into your thick
    head, you great ugly bumpkin!
Baldemar   Sing for me ... or die!

He snatches up the bowl and moves away

Amanda (*speaking, alarmed*) Don't walk away from me. Where are you
    going? You can't leave me here like this! Come back, do you hear me?
    Come back or I'll — Urrrgghh!

*She has moved forward too far, past the extent of her neck chain. The result
is that she nearly chokes herself*

The slamming of a large iron door

(*Speaking in a little voice*) You can't leave me down here like this. Please!
What am I going to do? (*She starts to go back into her dungeon*) What am
I going to do? Help! Help!

The Lights fade back to the garden

Robert and Belle are walking together

Robert   Surely your father's life cannot still be in danger?
Amanda (*half-sung, her voice from a distance*) Help!
Robert   The Beast must be satisfied now that he has Amanda?
Amanda (*her voice from a distance*) Help!
Belle   Who knows with Baldemar ———

She breaks off as Amanda's voice hits an uncharacteristically musical note

Amanda (*her tuneless voice from a distance*) Help!

Belle frowns

Robert   What is it?
Belle   I heard —
                                I could have sworn —
                                I thought I heard ...
(*Shaking her head*)   Nothing.
Robert   That's in the past.
                                You're now with me.
                                For ever safe ...
Belle (*smiling sadly*)   For ever after?
Robert   For ever after ...
Belle (*sadly*)   In the world I come from, Robert,
                                That story might be true.
                                Your world is very different.
                                A world where dreams are harder to achieve ...
Robert   You mean one day you'll leave me?
Belle   Or may be taken from you.
                                Who can tell?
                                I know too little of your world —
                                But just enough to tell
                                There are no clear beginnings.
                                Nor are there tidy, happy endings.
                                Your stories are confused.
                                A tragedy for some becomes
                                A comedy for others;
                                You laugh at sadness,
                                Weep when you should smile.
                                Evil does not always die
                                And virtue's rarely seen to be rewarded.
                                The bad sometimes are most admired;

The good the most ignored;
The weak are made to bow before the strong;
And no-one seems to be the way they seem;
And no-one means the words they mean to say;
When every look denies what's being said ...
This dream becomes a nightmare.

Robert (*trying to calm her*)
Belle, sweet Belle.
My gentle tender Belle.
Stay with me and I can promise
We can make this world our paradise.
Safe away from your cruel world
From those who only mean to harm you ...

Belle (*still upset*)   Then they don't in your world
Ever lock you away?
Ever starve you for days?
Ever threaten and shout just to scare you?
Ever shut out your light?
Ever freeze you with cold
In a dungeon half-flooded with water?

She stops as Robert holds her tightly to him

At this point Mel appears from the house. She remains in the shadows, watching them. She has changed back into her normal clothes again. She carries a few overnight things, evidently for her stay in the tree house

As they sing, Robert draws Belle gently into the summer house

They are watched throughout by Mel

Robert (*soothingly*)   While you're sleeping
I will keep you safely ...

Belle (*uncertainly*)   You'll keep me safe while I dream of you ...

Robert   ... sleep, sweet Beauty,
Dream your lover's dreams.

Belle   ... safe in my lover's arms

Both   If we've woken
Can this all be real?
To find perfection's
Not a dream.
Awake, asleep, let's stay inside our dream
And fill our nights with love ...

Mel stares after them for a second, then turns abruptly and climbs into her tree house

As she does so, the Lights again cross-fade to Baldemar's castle

Amanda comes out of her dungeon, still attached to her chain. She looks very much worse for wear

The following is spoken unless indicated

Amanda (*weakly*) Help! Help! Please help!

The clang of the iron door. Baldemar appears. He carries the plate of food

Dear God! Where have you been? I've been down here for ages. I need food. I'm starving to death. (*Miming*) Food! Give me food!

Baldemar holds the plate just out of her reach. Amanda strains on her chain, trying to reach it. Baldemar is amused

Food! (*To herself*) I'll murder him! I swear I'll kill him. (*Trying a different tack, meekly*) Please ... please ...

She kneels and looks at him as plaintively as she is able to look

Baldemar (*singing, slowly*)
If you want your supper, little linnet, you
must sing for it first.
Amanda (*wearily*) You must stop asking me to sing. I can't sing. For the millionth time, I can't sing. (*A sudden inspiration*) Would you like me to dance? I can dance. Look.

She clambers to her feet and executes a few rather poor dance steps, presumably intended to be vaguely erotic. Finally, she nearly chokes herself again her chain

Baldemar laughs

Oh yes, very funny. Ha! Ha! Ha! Ha! You huge, grotesque — plank.
Baldemar (*singing*)   Sing, little linnet. Tweet! Tweet! Tweet!
Amanda (*screaming*) For the last time, I cannot sing. I refuse to sing. If you want to communicate with me you will do so like a civilized being. You will speak to me and I will speak back. Is that clear? All right? I am tone

deaf. I have no singing voice. None! Listen. Tweet, tweet, tweet! Are you satisfied?

The following is sung unless otherwise indicated

Baldemar	Tweet! Tweet! Tweet!
Amanda (*discordantly*)	Tweet! Tweet! Tweet!
Baldemar	My little bird inside her cage
	Sang tweet, tweet, tweet!

He beckons to Amanda

Amanda (*speaking*) Oh, dear heavens. What is the point? (*Singing feebly and out of tune*)

	My little bird inside her ... (*She stops*)
Baldemar (*insistently*)	My little bird inside her cage
	Sang tweet, tweet, tweet!
Amanda (*badly*)	My little bird inside her cage
	Sang tweet, tweet, tweet!
Baldemar (*lustily*)	Enough to make my cheery heart
	Go beat, beat, beat.
Amanda (*echoing*)	Enough to make my cheery heart
	Go beat, beat, beat.
Baldemar	A merry tune to make my day
	Complete, 'plete, 'plete ...
Amanda (*tuneless as ever*)	
	A merry tune to make my day
	Complete, 'plete, 'plete ...

(*Speaking*) What a perfectly inane song ...

Baldemar	Enough to set the tapping of
	My feet, feet, feet ...
Amanda (*soldiering on*)	Enough to set the tapping of
	My feet, feet, feet ...

(*Speaking*) There now, are you satisfied? Heard enough?

Baldemar	I stood there and I marvelled at this miracle of song ...
	With a melody so beauteous I was forced to sing along ...

Baldemar waves at her to join in again

Amanda (*speaking*) Oh, dear God, I can't bear it ...

They commence a very discordant duet

Both   My little bird inside her cage
                          Sang tweet, tweet, tweet!
                          Enough to make my cheery heart
                          Go beat, beat, beat.
                          A merry tune to make my day
                          Complete, 'plete, 'plete ...
                          Enough to set the tapping of
                          My feet, feet, feet ...
Amanda (*speaking*) This is a nightmare ...

The big finish

Baldemar   I bent my knee to Nature, just to thank her for this treat
                          For each starling in the hedgerow
                          Every sparrow in the street ...
                          But although I live to ninety-five, I never shall repeat
                          That time I heard my little bird

Waving Amanda in again for a cacophonous finale

Both   Go tweet ... tweet ... tweet ... !

A silence. Baldemar looks rather shaken

Amanda (*speaking*) Well. I have to say that wasn't as bad as I thought it was
    going to be. Do you want me to sing some more?

*Baldemar makes a series of emphatic, negative grunts. He thrusts the plate
of food at Amanda*

    (*Speaking*) Oh, all right, suit yourself. Thank you very much. About time,
    too.

She goes back into her dungeon, singing to herself as she does so

                          My little bird inside her cage
                          Sang tweet, tweet, tweet ...
Baldemar (*practising speaking, with difficulty*) Hallo .. hallo ... A-B-C-D-
    (*As he goes off*) Hallo ... Hallo. One ... two ... three ...

He goes

The Lights change to the garden. Mel remains half-hidden in the tree house

Grayson enters from the direction of the house. He approaches the summer house

The sound of Robert and Belle singing wordlessly and ecstatically from within

The following is spoken unless indicated

Grayson (*tentatively*) ... I say, Robert. I say ...

The sounds grow louder. Grayson moves to the doorway

I say ... (*Looking in briefly*) Oh, Lord. Yes. I see. Sorry.

He moves away hastily, ever the gentleman. The lovers' musical noises grow louder

Grayson sets up his own counterpoint in an attempt to drown them out. A sort of military march, perhaps

Grayson (*singing*)   Um-pah, um-pah, um-pah, um-pah. (*Etc.*)

The climax is reached. Grayson is left humming on his own. He stops. He leaves it a second and then calls out again

Hallo. I say. Robert ...
Robert (*from within, ecstatically, singing*) Hallo ... (*Speaking*) I mean, hallo. Who is that?
Grayson It's Grayson. Sorry to interrupt.
Robert Just a second.

A moment and Robert comes out on to the veranda. There are signs that he has dressed in a hurry. He looks a little dazed

Hi!
Grayson Hallo.
Robert Yes. What?
Grayson I said, "Hallo".
Robert Oh, yes. Yes. Indeed, it is. What can I do for you?
Grayson (*rather confused*) — Er ... what was it? Oh, yes. It's the — bed.
Robert Bed?

Grayson Yes. For Belle. Chrissie wants us to move it. Belle's sleeping in Mel's room. Eventually. But apparently, Mel's bed isn't good enough for Belle. She wants us to move Mel's bed out and put the spare bed in for Belle. I'd have asked Sinclair only he's lying down. Crying.
Robert Ah. Right. I'll give you a hand.

Belle emerges behind Robert. She is wearing what appears to be his dressing-gown. She is smiling

Grayson Ah ...
Robert Belle's been ... I've just been showing Belle around the place.
Grayson Oh, good.
Robert She's been ... trying everything.
Grayson Yes?
Robert The frower ... the shidge ... fridge.
Grayson Yes. Well, they're all worth a shot, aren't they?

Slight pause

Robert I'll give you a hand.

The following is sung unless indicated

(*Tenderly to Belle*)	I have to go with Grayson.
	Wait here!
	I have to move a bed ...
Belle (*happily*)	Bed!

Robert and Grayson start to move off

Robert (*as they go*)	Wait there, my love ...
Belle	I'll wait ...
Rober	Wait there for me ...
Belle	I'll wait for ever ...
	Till the world no longer turns ...
Robert	Till the sun no longer burns ...
Both	I'll wait.
Robert (*to Grayson, speaking*)	Lead on.

Grayson and Robert go off. Belle stands alone on the veranda for a moment

Belle (*softly to herself*) Till the world no longer turns,
                                    Till the sun no longer burns ...

I'll wait —

On the last word her voice cracks slightly. Puzzled, she tries again

Wait ...

The result is worse. She tries to find the note, once or twice more

(*Vainly trying to sing*) Wait ... wait ... wait ...

A very distant rumble of thunder

From her tree house, Mel continues to watch

Belle goes inside, looking a little disturbed

As she goes, the Lights return to Baldemar's castle

The iron door clangs and Baldemar enters with another plate of food. He bangs it on the floor as before

Amanda (*speaking, off*) ... just a minute ...

There is the sound of her warming up her voice with a very unmusical scale. Baldemar winces and groans. He bangs the plate on the floor again

Amanda appears

(*Immediately, speaking*) Ah, now ... (*Singing, rapidly and tunelessly*)
             Now, I really must insist
             That if you keep me here like this,
             That I have tissues in the loo,
             That I have carpet on the floor,
             That something's done about the rats,
             That I have knives and forks and spoons,
             That there are cushions on the chairs,
             That there's a mattress on that bed,
             That I have proper linen sheets ——

Baldemar gives a bellow

(*Speaking*) Wait, I haven't finished ...(*Singing on, undeterred*)
             A decent pillow that is clean,

A proper toothbrush and a sponge,
That I can bath three times a week,
I want a change of underclothes,
I need my hair done twice a month,
I want some oil for this chain,
A moisturiser for my face,
Oh God, and something for my nails,
I want ...

Baldemar (*speaking*) BE QUIET!

The following is spoken unless indicated

Amanda (*startled*) What?

Baldemar (*with difficulty*) You — be — quiet ... woman.

Amanda Oh, so we're talking now, are we?

Baldemar Eat — food ...

Amanda Well, this is progress. What's brought about this change of heart, I wonder?

Baldemar Eat — food ...

Amanda Please. Eat food, *please*.

Baldemar Eat — food — please ...

Amanda That's better. (*Taking the plate*) Thank you.

Baldemar Thank you.

Amanda (*inspecting the plate*) Oh, yes, it's this again, is it? The chef's special. Not a lot of variety in your kitchen, is there? This could do with some kind of a sauce. A sauce piquant.

Baldemar Sauce ...

Amanda Yes. We'll get you on to that, shortly. (*Starting to eat*) And who knows, maybe even a knife and fork eventually. Knife and fork? My God, let's start with a table first, why not?

Amanda continues to eat. Baldemar hums to her softly

And we can do without the lunchtime recital, thank you. No music. I do not want music while I eat. No music, thank you.

Baldemar No — music ...

Amanda No music at all. No music. Nice and quiet. I do not like music. Ever. All right?

Baldemar No music?

Amanda Right. (*She finishes*) That's quite enough of that. (*Beckoning him*) Now come with me. Come on. I want to show you one or two things I would like doing. In here. Come on. Follow me.

Baldemar (*singing*) My little bird inside her ...

Amanda This way and no singing ...

Amanda goes off to the dungeon. Baldemar takes up her plate and follows her, rather bewildered by the turn of events

Baldemar (*as he goes*) No singing ...

The Lights change back to the garden. Mel climbs down from the tree house and moves towards the summer house. From within, the sound of Belle still trying her voice

Mel draws back into the shadows, crouching

Belle comes out on to the veranda. She is fully dressed again

She seems unhappy. She picks up the picture of her and Baldemar and stares at it sadly. Mel shifts uncomfortably and breaks a twig

Belle (*singing, without apparently looking at Mel, softly*)
                    Hallo. You must be Mel ...
Mel (*startled, then speaking abruptly*) Yes. (*Rather hostile*) What's it to
    you?

Mel makes to move on again, back to the tree house

Belle (*singing*)   Mel ... please don't go ...
Mel (*stopping*) Why? (*Staring at Belle*) Is it true what they say? You can only
    sing? You can't speak?

No reply from Belle

That you can only understand people if they sing at you?

No reply

That's a load of bollocks, isn't it? It's a joke. One of Robert's jokes. Brings
his bit down for the weekend, passes her off as a singing princess. That
right? Who are you anyway? He's never mentioned you. Mind you, why
should he? Nothing to do with me, is it? He can have who he wants. I don't
care.

A pause

See if I care.

A pause

I don't give a stuff, either way.

A pause

(*Angrily*) I just think it's a bit bloody much, turning me out of my bedroom, that's all ... just for you. OK. What do I matter, anyway? Get back in your cupboard, kid. Yes, sir, yes, ma'am. 'Night, 'night ...

Mel makes to go again, back to her tree house

Belle (*singing*)   Mel ... please stay ...
Mel (*irritated*) Why? What do you want?
Belle (*singing*)   Why do you hate me?
Mel (*speaking*) What are you talking about? I don't hate you.
Belle (*singing*)   Why do you hate me?
Mel I'm saying, I don't hate you. It's him I hate, if it's anyone. It's nothing
to do with you ... (*Shouting*) Go on, go away. Go and sing him to sleep.
Bugger off and leave me alone, all right?

Mel goes off for a second

Belle stands, still clasping her picture

Mel comes back, having calmed down slightly

(*After a pause*) I'm sorry. I don't know why I'm shouting at you. I'm sorry.
You're just another victim of that — bastard, aren't you? Probably a worse
victim than me, for all I know. It's not your fault. I'm sorry.

She touches Belle briefly. An awkward gesture of reconciliation

Sorry. Forget it, OK?

A silence, Mel sits. Belle sits beside her, remaining silent

It's just there are times when ... (*She stops*) There are times when ...
(*Starting to sing, gently at first, then building*)
                    There are times when
                    He seems to notice me
                    There are times when

He's standing close to me
It almost seems he needs to touch me.
He's going to smile at me and say
I think you're great, I think you're special,
You're just unique in every way ...
Yes, there are times.
There are times.

There are signs, too.
He likes my company.
When he seems pleased
To sit and talk to me.
A stupid joke, a pointless story,
A silly row between good friends.
A sort of casual acquaintance
Upon which not a lot depends ...
Then, there are times ...
There are times.

There are times when,
I yearn to cling to him.
Other times when
I ache to be with him.
To let him know how much I want him,
To throw away my senseless pride —
To stand before him quite defenceless
With not a feeling left to hide ...
Yes, there are times ...
There are times ...

But there's times when
He barely speaks to me.
There are times when
I'm close to hating him.
The way he mocks my every gesture —
And treats me like a child of two ...
I want to say goodbye and tell him
Our relationship is through ...
But then there's times,
There are times ...
There are other special, magic times ...

A silence

(*Speaking*) Why am I telling you this? (*Smiling*) Sorry. (*Singing*)
          Why am I telling you this?

Belle smiles but does not answer. The following is sung unless indicated

	Does he really love you?
Belle	He thinks he does.
	Which for a man,
	Means very much the same ...
Mel	And do you really love him?
Belle	I can't deny
	I love him, yes —
	But not as much as you ...
Mel (*despairingly*)	Then why ... ? Why?

During the next song, Belle will, almost unnoticed, stop singing and drop for the first time into normal speech. So absorbed are the two women, they appear for a time to be unaware of the change

Belle (*gently*)	Mel, understand.
	Try to understand ...
	Love has no rhyme nor reason,
	No set pattern, no fixed season.
	Love comes on love's own terms
	And lingers with her favoured few.
	Love leaves when love decides,
	Without farewells for somewhere new.
	Love holds back when she's bidden
	Keeps love's face both dark and hidden.
	Love enters unannounced.
	She teases those with whom she flirts.
	Love heals or love gives pain,
	Has no remorse for those she hurts.
	Love, though, you will discover,
	Love's a true, a constant lover.
	Love often can reward
	Those whose hearts are young and sure
	Love visits there (*speaking in rhythm*) but once
	And stays inside them, ever pure ...

Belle is now speaking, not singing. The following is spoken unless indicated

Mel It would be good enough to believe that, wouldn't it?

Belle Trust me. On this night of all nights, trust me.

Mel (*solemnly*) I do.

Belle More important, trust yourself, Mel.

Mel (*smiling*) Much, much more difficult. Anyway. It's all slightly academic, isn't it? I can't make him love me, can I? Not if he doesn't. Which he doesn't. Now, that is impossible ...

Belle Maybe he does ...

Mel He doesn't, I've told you he ——

Belle One day he will. How can he love anyone, while he hates himself? But he will. One day. You'll see.

Mel How could you know? How could you ever know that?

Belle Because I read the story.

Mel Story? What story?

Belle It's an old, old story.

Mel It may be just a story to you. It happens to be my life, mate ... (*She stops*) Wait a minute, we're talking.

Belle Yes.

Mel I mean, we're not singing?

Belle No.

Mel How come? I thought you could only —— ?

Belle I don't know. I don't know what's happening to me. I'm losing ... I'm losing the ——

Mel Losing what?

Belle My strength. It's being here, it must be. It's coming here. I betrayed my father, you see. And so I was sent here ... I promised to marry and I ran away ... I broke a vow ... and I'm being punished ...

Mel Punished?

Belle Yes ...

Mel By coming here?

Belle Yes.

Mel But how? Why here?

Belle Because ... because, where I come from we know this place as hell.

Mel Hell?

Belle I'm sorry.

Mel Here?

Belle I shouldn't have said it. Promise me you won't — promise.

Mel (*a bit shaken*) Well, I always thought it was pretty bad, but — you should see a few other places ...

Belle Mel, you won't say anything? Promise me you won't say anything, will you? You won't tell Robert? Please don't tell Robert.

Mel Why not?

Belle (*imploring*) Please. Please ...

Robert enters from the house

Robert (*cheerfully singing*)
                    Madam, we've moved your bed.
                    Grayson and I are half-dead.
                    He has a hernia and I've done my back in
                    Follow me now if you please
(*Speaking*) Hi, Mel.
Mel (*miserably*) Hi!
Robert I'm afraid we — Grayson and I — may have caused a bit of chaos.
In your room. Getting the bed in and out. Sorry.
Mel Treat the place as your own ...
Robert (*staring at her for a second*) OK. Thanks.
(*Singing, to Belle*)   Ready?
Belle Yes. Of course. Good-night, Mel.
Mel 'Night.
Robert Hey, you're talking.
Belle Yes.
Robert What's happened?
Belle I think my voice is a little tired, that's all.
Robert (*concerned*) Well, come on. Bedtime. What you need is rest ...

He starts to lead her off, gently

Belle Yes.
Robert You need your beauty sleep, that's what you need, don't you ... ?

He goes off laughing, escorting Belle

Mel sits unhappily watching them go. The Lights cross-fade again

We are back at Baldemar's castle

The clang of the iron door

*Amanda, now without her collar and chain, comes busily on. Behind her
trails a rather demoralized Baldemar. He is carrying several lengths of
timber and a saw*

Amanda (*briskly*) ... now it's perfectly simple. I want the shelves in this
alcove and then upstairs I need cupboards.
Baldemar ... cup-boards ...
Amanda Good deep cupboards. Come along, I'll show you. It won't take
you a second ...

Baldemar begins to sing to himself, rather mournfully

And no singing, please. What did I tell you about singing? How many more times?

Baldemar stops singing and follows Amanda off, unhappily

The Lights change again, back to the garden

Mel remains where she was. She is now crying quietly

Sinclair comes on from the house. He stands looking rather lost. He sees Mel

Sinclair Oh, hallo.

Mel ignores him

Just thought I'd ... in case ... Well, there's always a chance, isn't there? That he'd have — have — you know decided to sling her back. I mean, she's not the easiest of — it's not everyone who can ... I know that. I knew that when I married her. Everyone said to me at the time, Sinclair, you're a bloody fool. She'll have you for breakfast. She'll chew you into little pieces — she'll break your ... She'll break your spirit. But she hasn't, you know. I can't think why not for the life of me. But she hasn't. Not at all. I mean, first sign of a crisis I'm usually number one to go under. But you know, living with her, living with Amanda, it's actually done me good. I mean, there's never a dull moment, if you see what I mean. You can never relax, living with her, not for a second. Or she'll be on to you. In a flash. What are you doing? Why aren't you doing it? And you see I'm normally a man who relaxes all the time. That's been my problem. Slept through kindergarten, dozed through school, nodded off at university. But, being with her, well, it's like being on a perpetual outward bound course. If you know what I mean. Always on your mettle. Got to be. I mean, I have to say it. I think she's just terrific stuff. I have to say it. Lucky the damn man who's gone off with her, that's all. The rotten swine ... (*He chokes back a tear*) Sorry, there I go again. Sorry, I'd love to stay and chat. Excuse me. Sorry ...

He hurries off again in some confusion, back towards the house

Mel watches him go, too concerned with her own unhappiness to react. She sits on the summer house steps

The Lights cross-fade back to Baldemar's castle

Amanda appears at the tree house area, now re-lit and transformed into a castle balcony. From below, the sound of desultory hammering

Amanda How are you getting on? Have you nearly finished? I'm dying to see what you've done with the ——

Baldemar comes on from below her, looking very crestfallen. He carries one or two pieces of timber, very crudely nailed together, plus his hammer

What on earth is that meant to be?

Baldemar Cup-board ...

Amanda A cupboard. *That* is a cupboard? You call that a cupboard?

Baldemar Cup-board ...

Amanda Well, I don't call that a cupboard, I'm sorry. Do you know what I call that? I call that a mess. That's what I call that. A pathetic mess.

Baldemar (*unhappily*) Mess ...

Amanda Yes. I've never seen anything so pathetic. What are you? You're pathetic, aren't you? You're pathetic. You're not a man, you're just pathetic, aren't you?

Baldemar Path-etic ...

Amanda (*taking the timber from him, impatiently*) Come here. Give it here. Come on, come here. Give it to me.

Baldemar climbs the steps with his cupboard, rather reluctantly

That's it. Now, give me that hammer. What on earth have you been doing here? There's not a single nail in straight, is there? Well, we'll just have to pull it all apart and start again, won't we? We'll do it properly. I suppose I'll have to show you ...

Amanda begins, not inexpertly, to dismantle Baldemar's handiwork. He watches abjectly. He begins to keel, rocking to and fro with unhappiness

(*Struggling with her task*) And will you stop that wretched noise. How many more times?

She continues with her task. Baldemar slowly sinks to his knees, still moaning softly. He curls up into a ball. Amanda completes her task, unaware of this

(*Standing back, satisfied*) There. Now. I suppose I've got to teach you the basic art of hammering a nail into a piece of wood. No wonder this place is such a tip. I warn you, once I get started I've got a thousand little jobs for you to do ... (*She sees Baldemar for the first time. Slightly alarmed*) What's the matter? Get up at once. What's wrong with you?

Baldemar moans. A rumble of thunder as he does so

Oh, don't be so stupid. There's no point in sulking just because ...

Baldemar groans louder. Thunder and music

You're not ill, are you? You can't be ill? You can't get ill on me. What am I going to do if you're ill? You can't leave me stuck in this damn great castle all on my own ...

Baldemar lets out a loud cry of anguish

(*Running about agitatedly*) Oh, God. I say. Somebody, help! Do you have a doctor? No, of course you don't, you haven't even got a first-aid tin. Help! Somebody, help, please!

Amanda hurries off, leaving Baldemar curled up on the balcony, moaning

A bigger clap of thunder and music under, then torrential rain in the trees as we return to the garden

Mel, still on the summer house steps, is sitting unsheltered from the deluge

Belle, in a nightdress, comes running on, barefoot

Belle (*calling above the storm*) Baldemar! Baldemar!

Robert comes rushing on behind her

Robert Belle, what are you doing? For God's sake!
Belle (*calling again*) Baldemar!
Robert (*yelling above the storm*) Belle, it's pouring with rain. You'll catch pneumonia ...

More thunder and music, combined with another cry from Baldemar. Belle picks up the picture from the veranda

Belle (*calling, desperately*) Baldemar! I'm sorry! I love you! Take me back!
Robert Belle, what are you saying ... ?

Belle I love him, I love Baldemar. (*Calling*) Baldemar, take me back. Forgive me!

Robert (*seizing her*) Belle, what are you talking about? You love me. You don't love him. You don't love Baldemar. You love me.

Robert wrenches the picture from Belle and throws it back on the veranda. Another cry from Baldemar. More thunder and music

Belle Baldemar! I'm coming! (*Desperately*) He can't hear me! He can't hear me! He can't hear me, unless I sing — (*Trying in vain to sing*) Baldemar! Balde ... Balde ... (*In tears*) I can't sing, why can't I sing any more ... ?

She sinks to her knees on the grass. Robert kneels beside her

Robert (*as calmly as he can*) Belle ... listen to me ... Belle ... (*He grabs her shoulders*) Belle ...

Another cry from Baldemar, more thunder and music

Belle looks up anxiously

Forget him ... Forget Baldemar ... you understand?

Belle Robert, he's dying. Baldemar is dying ...

Baldemar cries. More thunder and music

Chrissie comes on in her nightclothes and a sou'wester, followed by Grayson similarly attired, but without a sou'wester, sheltering his head with a newspaper

Chrissie What's going on out here?

Grayson What the hell's the matter?

Robert (*waving them away*) It's all right. It's all right! Just a minute!

Chrissie But, Robert, what's happening?

Robert It's all right ...

Grayson What do you mean, it's all right? Both of you sitting out here in a force-nine gale and a major monsoon, what are you talking about?

Chrissie Mel, come inside at once, dear ...

Mel (*hugging herself, miserably*) Leave me alone ...

Robert (*shaking Belle to get her attention, urgently*) Belle, listen. Your life's with me now. With me. Do you see? You don't belong back there. Not any more. Forget it. Forget all of it. You're mine now, Belle. You belong to me, I belong to you. Don't you see that?

More thunder and music

Belle pulls away from Robert and rises

Belle No, no, no ...
Robert (*calling after her*) Belle, you belong here, now.

Belle moves further away

Belle (*more quietly*) Baldemar ...
Robert Belle ... (*He makes as if to follow her*)
Mel Robert! Forget her.
Robert (*startled, turning to her*) What?
Mel I said forget her. You're wrong. She doesn't belong here ...
Robert Listen, keep out of this, Mel.
Mel No, I won't keep out of it ...

Mel rises and stands between Robert and Belle

Robert, listen! Belle has no place here. She doesn't belong to you. She doesn't belong to anyone ...
Robert Get out of the way ...
Mel Do you know where Belle thinks she is, Robert? Where she believes herself to be? In hell. She believes she's in hell ...
Robert Oh, come on, don't talk childish rubbish ...
Mel It's true. This isn't paradise. Not for her, anyway. This is what she believes — what she's been brought up to believe — is hell. Don't you understand? She can never be happy here. Don't you see?

Robert looks at Belle who has turned to look at them

(*Slightly calmer*) She told me that herself. Ask her, Robert, ask her. Go on, ask her.
Robert (*after a slight pause*) Belle ... ?

More thunder and music

Belle looks up again. She goes into what appears to be a semi-trance like state

Belle (*softly*) Baldemar ... (*She continues to whisper his name to herself*)
Robert (*realizing this is the truth*) Oh, my God.

Robert slowly sits

Chrissie Would someone kindly tell me what on earth is happening?

Amanda comes back in the castle, now in a fine old state of panic

The wind is howling, lightning is flashing

Amanda ... stupid castle. I can't even get out of the front door. Baldemar!
How do I raise that portcullis? More important how do I lower that bloody
drawbridge ... ? Baldemar ... !

Amanda kneels beside Baldemar and tries to revive him

Mel (*to Chrissie*) The simple fact is, Mother, that Belle is trying to get back
where she came from. But for some reason, she can't.
Chrissie Why not? She got here all right.
Mel I don't know why not, I ——
Grayson Can't she — whatever she calls it — make a link, somehow. With
someone?
Mel I don't know. Possibly. (*Turning, calling*) Belle ... Belle ..
Belle (*coming out of her trance*) What?
Mel They're asking, can you make a link? Can you make a link with
Baldemar?
Belle I can't. He can't hear me ... unless I sing, he can't hear me. And I can't
sing any more ...
Grayson Well, what about him? Can't he sing?
Belle Baldemar's dying ...
Grayson Well, surely there's someone around the place who can sing, for
God's sake ... ?
Chrissie (*singing*) La — la — la — la ...
Grayson It's no good you singing, is it? Don't be so damn stupid, woman.
Amanda Baldemar ... for heaven's sake, wake up. Really, all this fuss over
a wretched cupboard. How do we get help? You must tell me, how can I
get help for you ... ? (*Imploringly*) Please, Baldemar ... please ...
Baldemar (*weakly*) Belle ...
Chrissie What if we all sang together?
Amanda What's that?
Baldemar (*a little stronger*) Call Belle ... !
Mel I don't think that would work, Mother ...
Amanda (*impatiently*) Baldemar, speak up, I can't hear you ...
Grayson It certainly wouldn't. Couple of choruses, we'll have the police
straight round again.
Baldemar (*with his remaining strength*) You must call Belle!

A huge clap of thunder and music. Belle screams as if in pain

Grayson What about Amanda? Could she make the link ... ?
Baldemar Sing ... Amanda ...
Robert Amanda?
Baldemar Amanda ...
Amanda What me? Sing?
Mel If she's there ...
Baldemar Sing ...
Grayson If she's still alive ...
Amanda What are you talking about? You've heard me singing ...
Chrissie Don't say that ... Of course she's alive ...
Baldemar You must sing ...
Robert Amanda won't sing. She can't sing ...
Amanda How can you expect me to sing ... ?
Grayson You never know. She might have a go ...
Amanda Don't be absurd ...
Robert Don't be ridiculous ...
Amanda You know I can't. I couldn't sing ...
Robert Amanda couldn't sing to save her life ...

Thunder. A weak, dying groan from Baldemar

Amanda Oh, what the hell! What have I got to lose?

Amanda opens her mouth and taking a deep breath comes out with the most amazingly pure, clear note

(*Speaking*) My God! Was that me?
Belle (*who has heard the note, excitedly, speaking*) Amanda!

Belle also draws breath. Together she and Amanda join notes

A whirl of light and sound

The women change places

Baldemar! (*She rushes to him*)
Amanda (*startled to find where she is*) Oh, hallo, everybody.
Chrissie (*overjoyed*) Amanda! Darling!

She thinks for a moment about embracing Amanda then thinks better of it. The others are equally cautious

Under the next, Belle begins to croon softly and wordlessly to Baldemar, cradling him in her arms and rocking him gently. The rain stops. The skies clear, though we remain in both places. The dawn starts

Grayson (*warily*) Welcome back, old girl ...

Mel (*likewise*) Welcome home ...

Amanda Oh, it's so good to be back, you've no idea. I've had the most appalling ... Oh, never mind. (*Seeing Robert, awkwardly*) Hallo, Robert ...

Robert (*likewise*) Hallo, Amanda ... I — never thought I'd say this, but it's good to see you ...

Amanda I — never thought I'd say this either but — it's almost a relief to see you, Robert.

They smile at each other. They start to move together

(*Suddenly, remembering*) But where's Sinclair ... ?

Amanda turns to the house

Where on earth's Sinclair? Sinclair ... !

Sinclair hurries on in night attire

Sinclair Amanda!

Amanda Sinclair!

Sinclair Amanda! Where have you been?

Amanda Where have you been?

Sinclair I'm sorry. I was asleep.

Amanda Asleep?

Sinclair Yes, I took a sleeping pill to try and forget you. And I'm afraid I fell asleep. Then I wake up and here you are. This is wonderful ..

Amanda (*hurling herself into his arms*) Oh, Sinclair ...

Sinclair (*surprised*) Oh. Yes. Jolly nice. Thank you.

Amanda is suddenly overcome with a lifetime's need for a really good cry. She does so for several seconds. The others stare aghast as they witness this hitherto unseen side to her. Sinclair is startled, then as he consoles her, grows almost masterful

Amanda (*recovering a little through her tears*) Sinclair. I can sing. Isn't it marvellous? I've learnt to sing.

Sinclair (*apprehensive again*) Oh, really ... Splendid.

Amanda Listen. (*She opens her mouth and sings*)

My little bird inside her cage
Sang tweet, tweet, tweet!
(*Speaking*) Come on, Sinclair. Join in!
Sinclair Oh, super. Yes. Right. Of course ...
Amanda (*singing*)   My little bird inside her cage ...

Sinclair joins in with Amanda tentatively at first, then starting to enjoy himself

Both (*singing*)   ... sang tweet, tweet, tweet ...
Enough to make my cheery heart
Go beat, beat, beat.
A merry tune to make my day
Complete, 'plete, 'plete ...
Chrissie (*speaking*) Oh, what fun ...

Chrissie joins in the singing. The following is sung unless indicated

The Three   Enough to set the tapping of
My feet, feet, feet ...
Amanda (*alone*) I bent my knee to Nature, just to thank her for this treat —
Chrissie (*speaking*) It's so good to see her happy, isn't it, Sinclair?
Amanda   For each starling in the hedgerow
Every sparrow in the street ...
Sinclair (*speaking, uncertainly*) Yes, it certainly is ...
Amanda   But although I live to ninety-five, I never shall repeat
That time I heard my little bird ...
Chrissie (*speaking*) Come on, Grayson ...

Grayson joins in

All Four   Go tweet, tweet ... tweet ... !
Chrissie (*speaking*) Oh, what fun ... Look, the sun's coming up. Come on, everyone. Breakfast on the lawn.
Amanda (*speaking enthusiastically*) Oh, yes ...
Grayson (*muttering*) Breakfast on the lawn? I'm not having breakfast on the lawn, it's covered in dew ——
Chrissie (*cutting him off as she starts to sing again*)
My little bird inside her cage
Sang tweet, tweet, tweet!

They all join in with her. Sinclair and Amanda enthusiastically, Grayson slightly less so. They all go off singing into the distance

Robert and Mel remain still until the voices die away. Belle continues to cradle Baldemar

All (*off, into the distance*)
>Enough to make my cheery heart
>Go beat, beat, beat.
>A merry tune to make my day
>Complete, 'plete, 'plete ...
>Enough to set the tapping of
>My feet, feet, feet ...
>I bent my knee to Nature, just to thank her for this treat
>For each starling in the hedgerow
>Every sparrow in the street ...

Over the end of this can be heard police sirens approaching the house

>But although I live to ninety-five, I never shall repeat
>That time I heard my little bird ...
>Go tweet ... tweet ...

The voices trail away, raggedly. The sirens stop. Robert looks at Mel, gives her a rather sheepish smile and moves towards the summer house. The following is spoken unless indicated

Mel You going to come up for breakfast?
Robert No, I have to pack ...
Mel What? Right now?
Robert Yes. I have a train to catch.

Robert goes into the summer house

Mel looks disconsolate. She waits, uncertainly. The following is sung

Belle (*softly*)   Baldemar ... Baldemar ...
Baldemar (*regaining consciousness*)
>I am sleeping
>For it's when I'm dreaming
>I find Beauty
>That's the way it seems.
Belle   You're not sleeping.
>You can reach and touch me.
>Beauty's with you
>Stepping out of your dreams

I am here for ever more, I promise not to leave you.
All I ask is you forgive and do not harm my father.
If you desire I will submit to go back in that dungeon.
To sit there in the dark in chains, it's all that I am ...

Baldemar   Never!

Mankind has no rightful duty
To enslave or fetter beauty,
Claim it as his own.

You are free to fly, sweet dove, I have no way to stop you.
If you stay it is your choice, it will be your decision.
For I have forfeited my claim. I kneel, I crave your pardon.
You'd live here, if you deigned to stay, a royal princess ...

Belle   Never!

Beauty has no right demanding
Privilege. No right commanding
Worship as her due ...

If I stay, I stay as neither slave nor master
If I stay, I stay as friend and loving partner ...

Baldemar   Once upon a time there was a legend long forgotten
That she who kisses this poor beast will have it in her
   power
To change him to a handsome prince

Belle   ... I have no wish to do so ...
The beauty that is in you now is more than I could ask for.

Both   If we've woken
Can this all be real?
To find perfection's
Not a dream.
Awake, asleep, let's stay inside our dream
And fill our nights with love ...

Beauty kisses the Beast

Meanwhile, in the garden, Mel waits patiently

   Robert comes out with a couple of cases

The following is spoken

Mel Do you need a hand?
Robert What?
Mel I said, do you need a hand?
Robert What's got into you all of a sudden?
Mel (*hurt*) OK, forget it. Forget I offered.
Robert (*softening*) Well, you can carry one of these if you like. Thanks.

Mel moves to the case but doesn't immediately pick it up. Robert seems on the point of going inside for the rest of his stuff

Mel (*off-hand*) I don't know why you're leaving, really.
Robert How do you mean?
Mel I mean, it seems to me the only reason you had to go was because of Amanda — and now — now she's changed, she seems to have forgiven you — there doesn't't seem to be any point in going. You might as well stay, mightn't you?
Robert I don't know. I think the prospect of an all-singing, all-dancing Amanda is even more daunting than the old one.
Mel (*still very casual*) Will you come back at all? To stay?
Robert I can't think of any reason to, can you?
Mel Well, there might be ...
Robert A reason?
Mel Yes.
Robert What reason?
Mel (*after a slight pause, shrugging*) I don't know ...
Robert I should think you lot will be glad to see the back of me, won't you? I'll get the rest of my stuff.
Mel (*anxious not to let him go*) Will you miss her?
Robert (*slightly irritable*) What?
Mel Will you miss her? Your princess? Are you upset she's gone?
Robert Yes. No, not in the way you think. No.
Mel In what way, then?
Robert You're probably too young to understand — but — you make a fool of yourself — you fall in love with a dream — some figment of your own stupid imagination ... an ideal .. a romantic illusion you could never hope to live with ... it makes you angry. Angry with yourself. That's all. Do you see?
Mel I'm not too young to understand that. Surprisingly.
Robert (*angrily*) Anyway, to hell with her. When she arrived here the first thing she told me was that I'd been sent to help her, she'd been sent to help me. What was all that meant to mean? I busted a gut trying to help her. And what's she done in return for me? Sweet nothing. No. We do it over and over again. All of us. We all fall for it — every time. If you take my advice, you'll stay up your tree. You'll be safe up there.

Mel (*with an angry cry*) That's not what I want!

Robert (*startled*) What?

Mel Nothing. Nothing.

Robert (*gently turning her face to him*) Listen, Mel. You're — you mean a lot to me, you know ...

Mel Yes?

Robert I'm really very fond of you — you've been a good friend. It's all right, I'm not trying to — I mean, I've grown very fond of you, that's all. Just with you being around, you know ... And I'm, I'm ... (*He hesitates*)

Mel Yes?

Robert Well, all I'm saying is — don't give anyone, lunatics like me for instance — especially lunatics like me — the opportunity to hurt you needlessly, OK? Never plunge into stupid, senseless, no-hope relationships. Never, never fall in love unless it's absolutely unavoidable. And never, never, never fall in love with the idea of love itself. Because, when it comes down to it, love is just one great big sexual propaganda trick, that's all. Put about by our hormones to fool our bodies into messing up our minds. Always follow your head, not your heart, all right?

Mel (*dully*) Yeah.

Robert seems for a minute to contemplate kissing her. Instead he settles for gripping her shoulders in a rather awkward way

Robert Sorry, I didn't mean to embarrass you. I know you hate all that ... Sorry.

He moves away from her and goes back into the summer house

Mel gives a little cry of frustration and rocks to and fro

(*Off*) What's that?

Mel Nothing.

She mooches on to the veranda. She picks up the picture

(*Doing her best to cope*) Don't forget your picture. This picture. Don't forget it.

Robert (*off*) God! That bloody picture. Have it. Take it. Please.

Mel What?

Robert (*off*) Hang it on your wall. Burn it for firewood. Give it to Grayson for Christmas. I don't want to see it again, I can tell you.

Mel (*drily to herself*) Thanks. Thanks a lot.

Robert (*off*) You want to start taking that lot up to the house. I'll follow on
  · in a minute.
Mel (*staring at the picture, whispering*) Belle ...
Robert (*off*) I'll phone for a taxi from here ...
Mel (*whispering*) Belle, Belle ... Help me. What am I going to do?
Robert (*off*) The last time I tried to order a taxi from here, it took about a week
  and a half to come ...
Mel (*very quietly, singing*)
             Belle ... Belle ... Help me ...

Belle stiffens as she hears Mel's voice. The following is sung unless indicated

             Help me ...
Belle   Mel, where are you?
Mel   Belle, I'm going to lose him.
             I just know I'm going to lose him,
             Belle, I need your help please ...
Robert (*off, speaking*) Mel, are you still there?
Mel (*speaking*) Yes.
Robert (*off, speaking*) What are you doing?
Mel (*speaking*) Nothing.(*Singing*)
             Belle, I'm going to lose him
             I swear I'm going to lose him,
             Belle, you need to help me ...
Belle   Mel, you have to talk, you have to say.
             You have to show, you must reveal,
             You mustn't hide, you can't conceal ...
Mel   Belle, you have to help me ...
Belle   Mel, you can't expect the man to guess,
             You can't assume he's second sight
             They're not that shrewd, they're not that bright ...
Mel (*in panic*)   Belle, you've got to help me ...

Robert comes out of the summer house with his remaining luggage

Robert (*speaking*) So? Where's all this offer to help?
Belle   Mel, you have to tell him ...
Robert (*speaking*) I carry them all myself, is that it?
Mel (*speaking*) No ...
Belle   You really have to tell him ...
Robert (*speaking*) OK, thanks. You take those, then. I'll take these. He'll
  come to the front of the house.
Mel (*speaking*) Right.

Belle   You're going to lose your chance, Mel ...
Mel   I know!
Robert (*speaking, puzzled*) What?
Mel (*speaking*) Nothing.
Belle   There's not a second chance, Mel ..
Robert (*speaking, stopping, concerned*) Are you all right?
Mel (*speaking*) Yes ...
Belle   This has to be the time, Mel ...
Robert (*speaking*) You look terrible ...
Belle   There are times, Mel ...
Mel (*speaking*) I know ...
Robert (*speaking, concerned*) Mel ...
Belle   There are times, Mel ...
Mel (*speaking*) I know, I know ... (*Singing*)
                                   I know!
Robert (*speaking, gently*) Mel, what is it?

Mel, with Robert's full attention, loses her nerve. Her mouth opens and shuts

Belle (*prompting her*) There are times ...
Mel (*falteringly*)   There are times ... (*She stops*)
Robert (*speaking*) What? What did you say?
Belle (*prompting her*) There are times ...

Mel hesitantly joins her

Both   There are times when
                                   You seemed to notice me.
                                   There were times when
                                   You stood so close to me
                                   It almost seemed that you would touch me.
                                   That you would smile at me and say

*Belle gently drops out and allows Mel to continue alone. Mel is now gaining
in confidence*

The Lights gently fade out on Belle and Baldemar

Mel   I think you're great, I think you're special,
                                   You're just unique in every way ...
                                   Yes, there were times.
                                   There were times.

There were signs, too,
You liked my company.
When you seemed pleased
To sit and talk to me.
A stupid joke, a pointless story,
A silly row between good friends.
A sort of casual acquaintance
Upon which not a lot depends ...
Then, there were times ...
There were times.

Robert is smiling at her

Robert   There's been times when,
I yearned to cling to you.
Other times when
I ached to be with you.
To let you know how much I loved you.

Mel   To throw away my senseless pride —

Robert   To stand before you quite defenceless

Mel   With not a feeling left to hide ...

Both   Yes, there were times ...
There were times ...

Mel   But there's times too
You barely spoke to me.

Robert   Then there's times when
I really hated you.

Mel   The way you mocked my every gesture —
As though I were a child of two ...
I nearly said goodbye and told you —
Our relationship was through ...

Both   But there were times,
There were times ...
And there'll be other special, magic, magic times.

Robert kisses her. Mel responds. They look at each other

Robert (*speaking*) You want to give me a hand with this luggage, then?
Mel (*speaking, apprehensive again*) To the taxi?
Robert (*speaking, smiling*) If you like. But then again, I think we'd do better
to put it all back in there again, don't you?

Mel gives a joyous whoop and embraces him. A surge of music

They grab up part of the luggage and go into the summer house together

Mel returns immediately jumping in the air in a mixture of triumph, joy and sheer relief. As she gathers up the rest of the luggage there is a Black-out

CURTAIN

FURNITURE AND PROPERTY LIST

ACT I

On stage: Small garden table. *Under it*: grip bag. *On it*: water-colour illustration of Beauty and the Beast pinned to a board; artist's materials including pencil, jam jar of paint water, paint brushes
2 or 3 chairs

Off stage: Buffet food wrapped in paper napkin (**Mel**)
Carrier bag containing full bottle of Scotch (**Robert**)
Glass of white wine (**Grayson**)
Duster (**Belle**)

ACT II

On stage: As before

Off stage: Small tree branch (**Sinclair**)
Bowl of food (**Baldemar**)
Overnight items (**Mel**)
Plate of food (**Baldemar**)
Several lengths of timber, saw (**Baldemar**)
Crudely nailed pieces of timber, hammer (**Baldemar**)
Newspaper (**Grayson**)
Cases (**Robert**)
Luggage (**Robert**)

Personal: **Amanda**: large steel collar with metal chain

LIGHTING PLOT

Practical fittings required: garden lights

ACT I

To open: Summer evening exterior; gradually becoming dark as act
progresses; practicals on, lighting in summer house

Cue 1	**Grayson**: "... in the ——" *Moonlight comes up*	(Page 26)
Cue 2	**Amanda**: "Please!" *Practicals and summer house lighting flicker*	(Page 41)
Cue 3	**Sinclair** collapses in a faint *Fade to black-out*	(Page 43)

ACT II

To open: Practicals on; exterior night effect

Cue 4	**Crash of music** *Change to gloomy, unreal lighting*	(Page 49)
Cue 5	**Amanda**: "Help! Help!" *Cross-fade to previous lighting*	(Page 50)
Cue 6	**Mel** climbs into the tree house *Change to gloomy, unreal lighting*	(Page 53)
Cue 7	**Baldemar** goes *Cross-fade to previous lighting*	(Page 56)
Cue 8	**Belle** goes back inside *Change to gloomy, unreal lighting*	(Page 58)
Cue 9	**Baldemar**: "No singing ..." *Cross-fade to previous lighting*	(Page 60)

Cue 10	**Mel** sits unhappily, watching them go *Change to gloomy, unreal lighting*	(Page 65)
Cue 11	**Baldemar** follows **Amanda** off unhappily *Cross-fade to previous lighting*	(Page 66)
Cue 12	**Mel** sits on the summer house steps *Change to gloomy, unreal lighting on the tree house area*	(Page 66)
Cue 13	**Baldemar** is curled up on the balcony, moaning *Cross-fade to previous lighting*	(Page 68)
Cue 14	**Chrissie**: " ... what on earth is happening?" *Change to gloomy, unreal lighting on castle area; lightning*	(Page 71)
Cue 15	**Belle** and **Amanda** join notes *Whirl of light*	(Page 72)
Cue 16	The rain stops *Increase all lighting; bring up dawn effect on garden,* *gradually increasing*	(Page 72)
Cue 17	**Mel** continues singing on her own *Gently fade lighting on* **Belle** *and* **Baldemar**	(Page 80)
Cue 18	**Mel** gathers up the rest of the luggage *Black-out*	(Page 82)

EFFECTS PLOT

ACT I

Cue 1	To open *Birdsong; occasional guests' voices etc., continue* *throughout act*	(Page 1)
Cue 2	**Grayson**: " ... get yourself fixed up ——" *Loud splash, commotion*	(Page 15)

ACT II

Cue 3	**Amanda** nearly chokes herself *Slamming of large iron door*	(Page 50)
Cue 4	**Amanda**: "Please help!" *Iron door clangs*	(Page 53)
Cue 5	**Belle**: "Wait ... wait ... wait ..." *Distant rumble of thunder*	(Page 58)
Cue 6	**Belle** goes *Iron door clangs*	(Page 58)
Cue 7	The Lights cross-fade to **Baldemar**'s castle *Iron door clangs*	(Page 65)
Cue 8	**Baldemar** moans *Rumble of thunder*	(Page 68)
Cue 9	**Baldemar** groans louder *Thunder*	(Page 68)
Cue 10	**Baldemar** is curled up on the balcony, moaning *Loud thunderclap; torrential rain in trees; continue*	(Page 68)
Cue 11	**Robert**: "You'll catch pneumonia ..." *Thunder*	(Page 68)
Cue 12	Another cry from **Baldemar** *Thunder*	(Page 69)

Cue 13	**Baldemar** cries *Thunder*	(Page 69)
Cue 14	Another cry from **Baldemar** *Thunder*	(Page 69)
Cue 15	**Baldemar** cries *Thunder*	(Page 69)
Cue 16	**Robert**: "Don't you see that?" *Thunder*	(Page 69)
Cue 17	**Robert**: "Belle ...?" *Thunder*	(Page 70)
Cue 18	**Amanda** comes back in the castle *Wind howls; continue*	(Page 71)
Cue 19	**Baldemar**: "You must call Belle!" *Huge thunderclap*	(Page 71)
Cue 20	**Robert**: "... to save her life ..." *Thunder*	(Page 72)
Cue 21	**Belle** and **Amanda** join notes *Whirl of sound*	(Page 72)
Cue 22	**Belle** cradles **Baldemar** in her arms *Rain stops, wind drops*	(Page 72)
Cue 23	**All** (singing in distance): "Every sparrow in the street ..." *Police sirens approaching*	(Page 75)
Cue 24	Voices trail away raggedly *Cut sirens*	(Page 75)